the Royal Marines
Total Fitness

the Royal Marines Total Fitness

The unique commando programme

Robin Eggar

Technical Advisers
Colour Sergeant Austin Woodin
Sergeant Dieter Loraine

VERMILION
LONDON

Dedication

To Captain Mark Wolsey and all the Young Officers from the batch, YO Sept. '91.

Thank you for welcoming a fat civvy into your lives, for sharing them with me and for setting a physical example that I felt compelled to follow.

To Jacqui, Jordan and Rowan who never begrudged the time spent.

Acknowledgements

This book would not have been possible without the tremendous assistance and input of all the Physical Training Staff at Lympstone Commando Training Centre, but extra special thanks are due to: Colour Sergeant 'Woody' Woodin and Sergeant Dieter Loraine for designing the exercises and adapting their basic Marine programme to civilian requirements, Sergeant Toby Broomes for starting my feet running and Captain Frank Allan for giving his permission.

At Lympstone CTC special thanks are due to: Camp Commandant, Colonel Mike Taffinder, who warned me that once I started with the Royal I might never leave; Major Matt Sturman of OTW for putting up with my intrusions; Sergeants Billy Baxter, Tom Coyle, Dai Phillips and Colour Sergeant Graham Foster of the batch training team for encouragement and abuse beyond the call of duty. And to all the other officers, NCOs, Marines, the staff of the Officers' Mess at Lympstone, not forgetting Captain Bill MacLennan of the Royal Marines Press Office in London, without whose help and encouragement I would never have been able to write this book . . . and enjoy it too.

Thanks are due to my agent, Julian Alexander, and Fiona MacIntyre at Vermilion who made me do it, and Jan Bowmer and Nicky Thompson who made it all work.

First published 1993 by Vermilion,
an imprint of Ebury Press, Random House UK Ltd,
Random House, 20 Vauxhall Bridge Road,
London SW1V 2SA.

ISBN 0–09–177699–6

Typeset by Hope Services (Abingdon) Ltd
Printed and bound in Great Britain by
Butler & Tanner, Frome and London

WARNING

If you have a medical condition, or are pregnant, you should not under any circumstances follow the programme in this book without first consulting your doctor. All guidelines and warnings should be read carefully and the author and publisher cannot accept responsibility for injuries or damage arising out of a failure to comply with the same.

Contents

Foreword

When I took 3 Commando Brigade to war in the South Atlantic in 1982, it was in the certain knowledge that they would cope with whatever challenges were thrown at them in what I knew would be a hard and possibly bloody struggle. I put this confidence down to the sure and certain knowledge that from the day they had walked through the gates of the Commando Training Centre, their training had been second to none. I was honoured with the privilege of commanding a force of men who were physically and more important, mentally, tuned to do almost anything. They in turn had complete confidence in their own abilities, none of which was misplaced. These men were not super-athletes. They had not been chosen for their prowess on the sporting field, nor were they born with any other special physical gifts. Before joining the Royal Marines, they were ordinary people like anybody else. What they all had in common was the self-motivation to succeed and the ability to keep going in conditions that would make others give up.

There are no secrets to Royal Marines training, no magic formulae. It originated in the hills around Achnacarry, in Scotland where Commandos trained during the Second World War. It is based on a combination of continuous mental motivation and progressively demanding physical training, always within reach of the individual, but always requiring him to strive to achieve it. The effort is made by the individual – nothing is achieved by aggressive instructors screaming at a recruit. By the time a Marine gains his green beret, his physical and mental fitness are matched superbly: he has achieved standards that he would have found unbelievable on the day he joined; consequently he is undaunted by challenges that would make many quail.

Not everyone can, or indeed wants to become a Royal Marines Commando, but everyone can benefit from the methods we use and our training ethos. This book is based upon the methods of training used by the Royal Marines Commandos, the knowledge and experience passed on by instructors and the experience of Robin Eggar, who undertook much of the training first hand. But no matter what level of fitness you strive for, whether it is to compete for your country in the next Olympic Games, or simply to be more able to cope with the stresses and strains of modern life, everyone can benefit from a little bit of the 'Commando Spirit'.

Major General Julian Thompson CB OBE
President of the British Association of Physical Training

This bronze 'Yomper' statue by eminent British sculptor Philip Jackson was unveiled at the Royal Marines Museum in Eastney, near Portsmouth, in 1992. The twice life-size sculpture, weighing about 3 tons, took just over 6 months to complete and was commissioned in tribute to the yomp by the Marines across the Falkland Islands in 1982.
Picture by A. L. Campbell, Dept of the Commandant General, Royal Marines

Introduction

Before you embark on the Royal Marines Total Fitness Programme, it might help you anticipate what to expect, if I explain what happened to me. I'd actually cracked the 30 Miler – of which more below – but I didn't know it. Inside my mind, where black clouds of failure were threatening to overwhelm my brain, it was the exact opposite. Instead of being a relief, after miles of Dartmoor hill and dale, the tarmac road I was running on seemed to stretch into infinity; the 20 plus pounds of weight in my pouches were getting heavier with each diminishing stride and no matter how far I ran I felt I was getting nowhere. I'd hit the wall – the point where you feel you cannot go on. My body was collapsing and my expectations and arrogance were shattered.

At times like that one starts to ask 'Why?'. Why does a thirty-seven-year-old civilian try to emulate the feats of a group of Royal Marine Officers in training? They are after all, on average, fifteen years younger and a light year or three fitter. All those young eyes the evening before had obviously been looking at me, confident in my hubris, with pity or disbelief. OK, so I had decided to chronicle their fifteen months of training but why add injury to insult and volunteer to do their Commando Tests? Pride, I guess. Pride augmented by a healthy dose of fear. Both fear of failure and fear of growing older, of not being able to prevent the slide into being out of time, out of shape and out of all my clothes.

So it was pride and fear that were responsible, that had led me to that road in the middle of Dartmoor on a warm June morning. Twenty of the 30 miles were already over but my pace was not up to that of the Marine officers. I had dropped behind first one – then a second – syndicate and now I was alone and deeply miserable. My brain kept telling my legs what to do, and although it seemed impossible they did comply, after a fashion. At the bottom of a gentle slope, I crossed a bridge just before beginning the steep hairpin ascent to the final checkpoint and the approach to Heartbreak Hill. The sun came out as I shuffled over the bridge, reflecting a rainbow off a clear pool of deep water. 'I don't have to do this,' I screamed, 'What am I doing? Why don't I take off all my hot sweaty clothes and dive into the water?' But instead of doing just that I laughed long and loud to the surprise of myself and

Running the last few hundred yards of the 30 Miler, aided and abetted by RMS Billy Baxter, was the culmination of 5 months' training for author Robin Eggar. He remembers: 'I forgot how close I had come to jacking it all in. That all came back to me when I was celebrating in the pub 3 hours later and my legs flatly refused to take me even as far as the bar.'

anything within earshot. And with that laugh I stepped over the wall. That was the moment I knew I was going to finish. Later on I discovered that I had not been alone in contemplating the lure of the pool – at least a third of the young officers had had similar thoughts.

Running that 30 Miler is the single physical achievement I am most proud of – and that is because I made myself do it. Nobody else. Most impartial observers, including many of the Marines, reckoned I didn't have a hope.

The 30 Miler comes on the third and final day of the Commando Test Week, less than 24 hours after a 9 Mile Speed March which has to be completed in under 90 minutes. On the first day, the Marines have 13 minutes to finish the Tarzan-Assault, a gruelling aerial assault course followed in the afternoon by the Endurance Course (2 miles in kit through mud and tunnels followed by a 4 mile run back to camp in under 72 minutes). The 30 Miler is more than just a cross-country run. Dressed in full combat gear, carrying 22 pounds of kit and a rifle weighing another 10 lbs a young recruit has only eight hours to cross Dartmoor in unpredictable weather conditions varying from blazing hot to freezing hail – and sometimes both. It is the final hurdle over which a young man must triumph before he earns the green beret of a Royal Marine Commando.

Only thirty weeks before this last test, this young man was just another civilian – probably fairly fit but nothing special. Now he is capable of carrying out rigorous, physically demanding tasks that would have many professional athletes crying out for mercy. Through years of trials and experience the Marines have developed a physical training regime that works on people of all heights and builds. Their aim is to create men who have built up their physical strength and flexibility so they can endure marching for miles while carrying heavy packs. The majority of Marines remain fit for life, because each has acquired the mental toughness and discipline necessary to do so.

When I decided to tackle some of the Commando Tests, I knew that it was not going to be easy and that I had to undertake a serious training regime. To the Marines I was just another 'fat civvy knacker bastard' – I certainly was and probably still am – but they have had years of experience at training the subspecies of humanity into trained Commandos. Desperate for some of that experience, I spoke to various Marine Physical Training Instructors at Lympstone Commando Training Centre in Devon. Sgt. Toby Broomes gave form to the crude running/cycling regime I had developed at home and on a painfully memorable March afternoon Sgt. Dieter Loraine introduced me to my Personal Individual Circuit. There are days when I still hate him for it.

That was the genesis for this book. As I trained towards the 30 Miler, Dieter and Colour Sgt. 'Woody' Woodin refined and adapted their exercise programme to my civilian needs. A great deal of the Royal Marines physical training is carried out on ropes – both high vertical climbs and horizontal crawls over tanks filled with water – culminating in the combined Tarzan-Assault Commando Test. Rope work is extremely good for working on upper body strength without building up excess muscle. However it is something that is virtually impossible to duplicate in civilian life and should never be carried out without a qualified instructor supervising at all times because of the danger of injury. Accordingly the PTIs devised alternative Commando Tests that will place you under just as much physical strain but can be carried out even by those suffering from acute vertigo!

So, what you have in your hands is unique – a tried and tested military formula specially adapted for civilian life. I know it works because I've done it for real. Twice. Fair enough, you may say. But what's in it for you? Why should you do this?

Let us assume that the idealized body shape for a man is to have strong muscular legs, a slim waist, powerful stomach muscles, all over muscle tone and tremendous upper body strength, all achieved without having Arnold Schwarzenegger biceps. Although many men dream of getting into such good shape, most work in sedentary civilian life, sitting in offices and taking sporadic exercise while their upper bodies thicken up and the inch of spare tyre around their bellies becomes a fistful. Yet it is not impossible for slothful fat civvies to become fit and to re-shape their thickening bodies into the ideal shape. However, dreaming of a miracle will not make it happen; just like everything else in life you have to work at it. You have to have a goal. When I topped the scales at 14 stone I knew that, as someone who enjoys the good things in life, if I didn't do something about it soon within ten years I would be carrying another extra stone of lard, a potential heart problem and an even harder physical task. That was my motivation – not forgetting pride, of course – and it was enough for me.

I worked hard at it and I changed on both the outside and the inside – where it matters more. Like most people, I have flirted over the years with a variety of exercise programmes, attended the gym sporadically and tried to take up *tai chi* but eventually external factors would conspire, I'd lose interest and drift into something else. That will never happen again. A few weeks after completing the 30 Miler I incurred a serious injury thanks to a pothole in a pavement, tearing the muscles off my Achilles tendon. After five weeks in plaster and intensive physiotherapy treatment I was unable to train properly for nearly three months – a good four weeks ahead of the most pessimistic prognosis. When I started again I was right back to Level 3 of the Royal Marines Total Fitness Programme and on the days scheduled for a jog it never seemed to stop raining. But on this occasion, for the first time in my life, I was not prepared to give up.

Reading this book will not automatically turn you into Apollo but it can help you change the way you feel about yourself. Being fit does enhance your lifestyle – this isn't American psycho-babble – and sharpens your mind, which helps at work. In a way, exercise acts as a pressure valve, letting the steam out of business or personal problems. The programme is not designed to be an all-consuming obsession, so start it when you are ready and always keep it in proportion. A Marine recruit has thirty weeks of training – an officer has fifty-four weeks – but they have much else to learn about the art of soldiering than simply getting fit. The Royal Marines Total Fitness Programme can be completed in sixteen weeks, but it should complement rather than dominate your life. If, for example, you know that the next three months are going to be hellishly busy with business or personal commitments, wait until your life is less hectic before starting the new regime.

Depending on how fit you are to begin with, the Royal Marines Total Fitness Programme starts gradually and initially only asks for an average 30–45 minutes commitment each day. So exercise can take place either before or after work – or even during the lunch hour – without destroying your social life. However, do be warned that as the Levels progress you will be carrying out increasingly gruelling physical tasks – though hopefully by then a 4 mile run, followed by 8 miles on a bike, a 40 minute Yomp and 20 Bastards (don't ask, all will be revealed later) won't seem too much. Not everyone will want to take it that far. So if after nine weeks, say, you feel enough is enough and that you have reached your physical peak, don't be disheartened or feel that you're a failure. Simply look in the mirror and there your progress will be revealed. Then turn to pages 111–113 which will tell you how to exercise to maintain your current level of fitness until you decide you want to continue.

Of course, I can preach and extol the virtues of the Royal Marines Total Fitness Programme until the last sheep leaves Dartmoor, but in the end it is out of my hands and into yours. It worked for me and it can work for you too. So I have only one final piece of advice. Remember that the programme is not designed to torture innocent civilians. So have fun, enjoy yourself and I'll see you on Dartmoor!

Robin Eggar
December 1992

How to Use This Book

The Royal Marines Total Fitness Programme is designed to take a 'fat civvy' (which is how the Marines refer to all new recruits whatever their physical shape) from lolling on his living room couch, drinking beer and eating chips to being able to pass some extremely stringent physical tests in only sixteen weeks. Even if you consider yourself quite fit, it is essential that you follow the instructions below. The key to the programme is that you must build up your physical strength gradually. If you cheat and move on to the next Level before you should, only you are to blame for any injury you may incur.

The programme comprises five fitness levels – each lasting three weeks – preceded by a preparatory week (J Week). Before you start the programme you will be asked to complete questionnaires on your health, lifestyle and physical condition, as well as taking an Initial Fitness Test which will determine your level of capability.

To get the major benefits of the programme please follow these instructions:

1 Complete the questionnaires on pages 18–21. Then move on to the Initial Fitness Test (page 21), which is in two parts. If you are in any doubt about your physical condition, consult a doctor before taking the Initial Fitness Test.

2 After taking the Initial Fitness Test, your combined test scores will show which of the five fitness levels you should join.

3 For the Marines, training is not just about physical fitness, it also involves acquiring a mental toughness so they can endure extreme hardship and discomfort. The chapter on Motivation (page 29) and the tips on motivation – based on personal experience – throughout the book will help to concentrate your mind and give you the encouragement you will need. Read about Motivation before you begin the exercise programme.

4 Before starting on your Level, you *must* undergo J Week (page 37). As well as preparing your body for the exercises to come, the J Week chapter contains vitally important details about the kit you require, gives detailed warm-up and stretching routines, as well as an introduction to the Individual Circuit which is the core of the book. **Don't miss out J Week**.

5 When you have completed J Week, move on to the Level you should be starting at – as determined by the Initial Fitness Test – and follow the weekly routines. Only move up a Level when you have passed the relevant Tests at the end of the Level you are at. If you are not ready to move on to the next Level, repeat the third week in that Level until you successfully complete the Test.

6 The programme culminates in the Commando Test Week (pages 107–109). This will prove how tough you really are – both mentally and physically.

7 Staying Fit (pages 111–113) gives guidance on how to maintain your fitness after you have completed the Royal Marines Total Fitness Programme.

8 Refer to pages 115–144 for extra information on diet, alternative exercises and tips on how to avoid injury.

Your Trainers

Colour Sergeant 'Woody' Woodin *(left)* and Sergeant Dieter Loraine *(right)* have been in the Royal Marines for many years, qualifying as Physical Training Instructors in 1978 and 1985 respectively.

As experienced, expert instructors they have trained countless recruits and potential PT instructors between them.
In addition to these duties, they have represented both the Royal Navy and the Royal Marines in sporting events, displays and competitions.

How Fit Are You?

Before he is selected as a recruit, every potential Marine has to go through a medical and various other tests to prove his suitability for the role he is undertaking. This chapter is similar in that it requires you to answer questions about your body and consider your approach to physical fitness. Some of the points here may only make more sense later on. Referring back to this chapter will give you a constant guide to how your physical shape and fitness are changing together as you complete the Levels in the programme.

However, you should remember that, while all body types can be improved to an extent, there is a finite level of improvement which everyone has to accept. The commonly held view is that physical ability is 75 per cent genetic and 25 per cent training and environment. So if you were born well rounded and have problems keeping your weight down, while exercise will help tremendously it cannot transform your basic body type. What exercise can do is help you improve your willpower – something the Marines have in abundance.

Men and women have a different body composition. The average male is 6 inches taller and heavier than the average woman, with 42 per cent muscle (against 36 per cent), 12–14 per cent fat (against 20–24 per cent) and 4 per cent more water. A suitably useless fact is that, because of their lower fat content, men will never make such good synchronized swimmers as women. Simply put, they can't float as well!

Although the Royal Marines Total Fitness Programme has been designed primarily with men in mind, there is nothing in the training programme – with the possible exception of the Commando Test Load Carry – that cannot be carried out successfully by a woman. The US Marine Corps now have female Combat Marines, the Royal Marines have started to accept female musicians and many member of the Corps – of all ranks – believe that there will be a woman wearing the Commando green beret within the next decade. However, do not attempt to undertake this programme if you are pregnant!

For advice on dietary matters, and tips on the best foods to eat for energy, see pages 115–119.

Smoking

Medical reports on the problems associated with smoking are well publicized – and ignored by dedicated smokers. Apart from the fact that smoking a packet of cigarettes a day doubles the risk of heart disease, when a smoker does any kind of physical exercise his performance is impaired because his body requires more oxygen and his heart beats faster. Therefore exercise is probably more important for a smoker than a non-smoker because to some extent it will help improve some of the physical deficiencies created by the habit.

If you are a smoker and don't want to give up that is a matter of personal choice. There are plenty of Marines who smoke, though many less than a decade ago. However, certainly in the initial stages of training, you will find some of the running and short stamina exercises much harder if you smoke.

Drinking

Doctors recommend that the average male should drink a maximum of 21 units of alcohol a week (and a woman 14 units). A unit is the equivalent of ½ pint of ordinary beer, lager or cider; ¼ pint of strong beer, lager or cider; a small glass of wine; or a pub measure of spirits. In the Marines, like many businesses, drinking is a social recreation and I would be a killjoy and a hypocrite if I suggested cutting it out all together.

However, particularly in the initial stages of the Royal Marines Total Fitness Programme, it's best to take it easy on the booze. While running off a hangover does work, throwing up in the street is both embarrassing and anti-social. So be sensible and try not to over-exert your body if you have had a few drinks.

Part One:
General Questions

First answer the following questions to the best of your ability. Keep a note of your weight, pinches and measurements so that you can refer to them later on.

1 Physical measurements

Potential Marine recruits are asked to supply general information and personal details such as their date of birth and marital status. Before you start the Total Fitness Programme, note down the following:

- Age   17
- Height
- Weight
- Measure these parts of your body and keep a record of the widest measurements:
  Stomach
  Thighs
  Chest
  Biceps
  Calves
- Do the fat test. Most gyms can do a proper test with calipers and charts but you can do the pinch test as an alternative. Take a pinch of flesh between thumb and forefinger in the following four places and measure the pinch:
- Biceps
- Triceps
- Beneath the shoulder blade
- 1 inch above and along from the hip bone

This is only a rough guide but when in the weeks to come you re-pinch the same places, you will notice a difference.

2 Look in the mirror. What do you see? What is your physical shape?

There are three basic body types. Are you:

- An ectomorph (long and lean with narrow shoulders and hips)   ☐
- A mesomorph (strong and muscular with broad shoulders and narrow hips)   ☐
- An endomorph (short with wide hips, round hips and a round face)   ☐

Ectomorphs make good long distance runners, but can have problems carrying weight over distances. Mesomorphs make good weightlifters and swimmers. Endomorphs have the problem that they can gain weight easily and even when not overweight look rounded . . . and cuddly.

Don't worry if you don't fit neatly into any of the basic types; many people are a combination and each has its advantages and drawbacks for the training you are about to undergo.

3 Lifestyle

a) Do you drink, if so how much and how regularly?

- A pint of beer/glass of wine ☐   • Once a week ☐
- Several pints ☐   • 2–3 times a week ☐
- Over a bottle of wine or   • Every day ☐
  equivalent ☐

b) Do you smoke
- No ☐
- The odd cigarette ☐
- Under 20 a day ☐
- Over 20 a day ☐

c) What is the basic constituent of your diet?
- Beer, chips and more beer ☐
- Meat and two vegetables ☑
- Chicken, fish, pasta and plenty of fibre ☐
- Vegetarian ☐
- Macrobiotic ☐

d) Do you or have you tried to diet in the past? How successful *NO* were you?
- Very successful ☐
- Fairly pleased with the result ☐
- A failure ☐

4 Exercise

Before you embark on the programme, think about how much exercise you already put your body through.

a) Do you take regular exercise?

Yes ☐
No ☑

b) How much do you exercise?
- Never ☑
- Once a week ☐
- 1–3 times a week ☐
- More than 3 times a week ☐

c) Were you fitter:
  - 5 years ago ☑
  - 10 years ago ☐
  - Longer ago than you care to admit even to yourself ☐

5 Motivation
- Why do you want to get fit? ☑
- Did you buy this book, or did someone give it to you? ☑
- Do you believe that this book will make you fit, or will you make yourself fit? ☑

Think about your answers. Ticking the various boxes does not give you a score which tells you how to become super fit in the next sixteen weeks. What they are doing is asking you to hold a mirror up to your body, to study your lifestyle and make a note of what you really see – not the perfect Adonis you want to see. If you are honest what you will almost certainly see is a physical body in need of improvement. Now the rest is up to you. There is no correct answer, no easy way to get fit. You have to want to do it.

Part Two:
Pre-Exercise Medical Questionnaire

You MUST answer Yes or No to the following questions:

	YES	NO
1 Has your doctor ever said you have heart disease or any other cardiovascular problem?	☐	☑
2 Is there a history of heart disease in your family?	☐	☐
3 Has your doctor ever said you have high blood pressure?	☐	☑
4 Do you ever have pains in your chest after minimal exertion?	☐	☐
5 Do you often get headaches, feel faint or dizzy?	☐	☑
6 Do you suffer from pain or limited movement in any joints		

	YES	NO
or bones which has either been aggravated by exercise or which might be made worse by it?	☐	☑
7 Are you currently taking drugs or medication or recuperating from a recent illness or operation?	☐	☑
8 Do you have any other condition which might affect your ability to participate in exercise?	☐	☑
9 Are you over 35?	☐	☑
10 Are you unaccustomed to physical exercise?	☑	☐

If you answered YES to any of these questions, consult your doctor BEFORE taking the Initial Fitness Test. Ask his or her advice as to whether you can undertake unrestricted physical training/activity on a gradually increasing basis. If your doctor suggests only restricted or supervised activities for an initial period ask whether the Royal Marines Total Fitness Programme fulfils these criteria.

If you answered NO to all the questions you should feel reasonably assured that you are suitable to take the Initial Fitness Test before passing on to the Total Fitness Programme.

However if you have a temporary illness, even as seemingly minor as a case of the snuffles, a cough or a slight sore throat POSTPONE taking the test until you are fully recovered. Don't be a macho fool.

Part Three:
Initial Fitness Test

You are now ready to take the Initial Fitness Test (IFT) which is divided into two parts. The IFT will determine just how fit you really are – this may come as a bit of a shock! You will need a pair of training shoes, a stopwatch and pen and paper to jot down the points you score, and some exercise clothes – a tracksuit to warm up in, and a T-shirt and shorts that allow you to move freely. Also, one of the exercises in Part One makes use of a sturdy chair.

The Test is divided into two parts, both are to be completed within an hour. The first part consists of 4 Circuit Exercises, the second a 1½ mile run. Wherever possible do the run on a training track or a properly measured route. At the end of the IFT, your combined score will enable you to calculate your fitness level.

Marines invariably have a giant Physical Training Instructor, with muscles like rocks and a vocabulary packed with inventive slang which he uses to encourage the more desultory members of the troop. You don't have a personal PTI. So whenever possible try to conduct all the tests in this book with somebody – a friend, partner or relative you can blackmail or coerce – standing by to time you, thus making sure you do the exercises properly.

Part One

Follow the instructions and photographs on pages 24–27. Count – out loud, if it helps – the repetitions of the exercises as you go along, and note the number of points earned after each exercise. Take no more than 2 minutes rest between each set of exercises in this part.

Do each exercise strictly, deliberately and slowly. Try to avoid cheating. Build up your momentum, thereby increasing the number of repetitions.

NOTE: If you have conducted Part One without any supervision, deduct 10 per cent from your score immediately for subconscious – and not always that subconscious – cheating. (Almost certainly you will not have carried out one of the exercises properly. A common shortcut is with press-ups – trying to get away with not letting the chest touch the ground each time.) If you don't like it, do another 10 press-ups. If you manage these, you can keep your original score.

TOTAL SCORE PART ONE = ~~59~~ 76.5 ....

Part Two

After completing Part One you may rest for not more than 20 minutes – then go on to Part Two. This test is a 1½ mile run in training shoes at your best pace. Walking and rests are allowed but the overall time recorded must include any such breaks. Remember to set a stop watch when you start running.

Before starting your run, provided you are still warm after Part One, do some light stretching for 5 minutes. If you .are not warm, do a 5 minute warm-up plus a quick jog (see pages 39–57). This will help you go faster.

Check how well you did on the run, allocating points as given below:

Over 14 minutes:	30 points
13–14 minutes:	40 points
12–13 minutes:	50 points
11–12 minutes:	60 points
10–11 minutes:	70 points
9–10 minutes:	80 points
Under 9 minutes:	90 points

TOTAL SCORE PART TWO = *80 pts*

What is your fitness level?

Add the points you scored in Part One and Part Two together to find what Level of the programme you are fit enough to tackle.

TOTAL SCORE ON INITIAL FITNESS TEST =

Over 70 points:	Level 1 – Couch potato
Over 100 points:	Level 2 – Civilian
Over 130 points:	Level 3 – Nod
Over 160 points:	Level 4 – Marine
Over 200 points:	Level 5 – Commando

NOTE: If you are only 5 points above the level marker, sorry but you have to drop down to the lower level. If you've scored 105 points, for instance, you have to start at Level 1, not Level 2. Life's a bitch, but at least you don't have to polish your boots after wading through waist-high mud. Seriously, if you are planning to exercise properly it is far better to take your time and not place undue strain on a body unused to such things.

Now you have found your level of fitness. However do not head straight for the relevant chapter. The next step is to undergo J Week. This is essential for it contains all the information you will need over the following weeks. Everybody must make sure that they are warming up and stretching properly. And even if you are already on the Commando Level you will have to learn how to test and prepare your individual circuits.

Don't worry if you feel a bit daunted or disappointed with your results in the IFT. Reading the next chapter on Motivation should make you feel more confident and ready to approach the challenges that lie ahead.

Sit-Ups

● Lie flat on your back with knees bent and feet flat on floor (fixed under chair or bar if necessary or with toes raised). Place your hands to the sides of your head (on temples). Do not place hands behind your head as this strains the neck and puts pressure on the base of the spine.

● Sit up to right angle then lie back to starting position.

Time 30 seconds.

Points 1 point per sit up.

Press-Ups

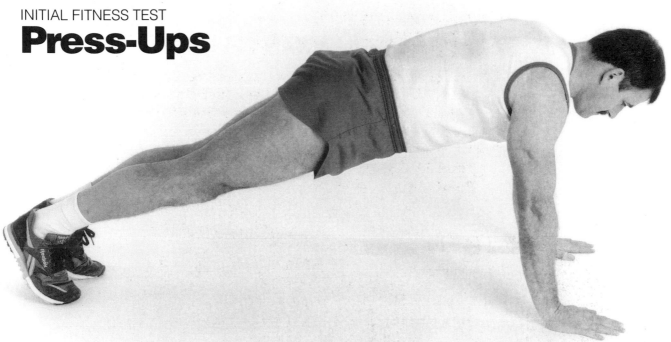

● Lie face down, hands shoulder-width apart, palms flat on floor and facing forwards. Keeping your legs and body straight, straighten your arms (but do not lock them) and push yourself up into the starting position so that only your hands and the balls of your feet touch the floor. Your head should be in line with your body.

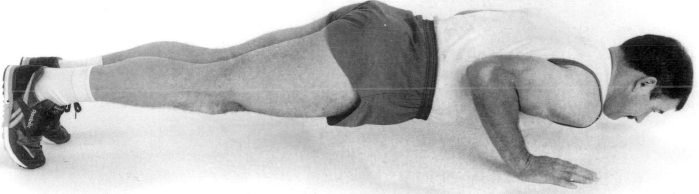

● Keeping your back straight, bend your arms and lower your chest to floor. Then, using the strength of your arms, push yourself back up to the starting position. Continue to lower and raise the chest making sure your chest just touches the floor with each repetition.

Time No limit. Keep going until you cannot continue – to a maximum of 30.

Points 1 point per properly completed press-up.

Squat Thrusts

● Start face down, hands shoulder-width apart, legs and body straight, head in line with body (as in press-ups position). Only the palms of your hands and the balls of your feet touch the floor.

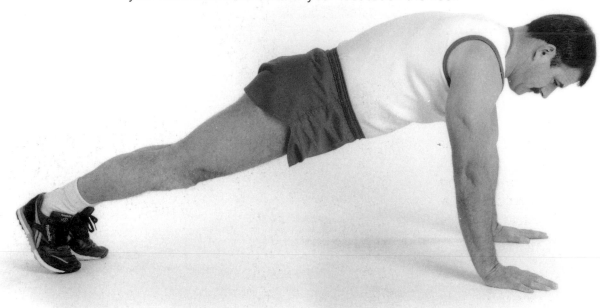

● Shoot both legs forward in a thrusting motion to where the knees are in line with the elbows and then thrust them back to the starting position with legs fully extended. Keep your bottom down and your back straight throughout.
Time 30 seconds.
Points 1 point per repetition.

Dips

- Sit on the edge of a sturdy chair, hands facing forwards and resting on the edge of the seat. Keeping your knees bent and your feet flat on the floor, move your torso and knees forwards so your bottom comes off the chair and your weight is supported on your hands.

- Using your arms for support, flex the elbows so that your bottom is lowered towards floor but does not touch it. Straighten your arms (but do not lock them) to lift yourself back up. Repeat, keeping your back straight throughout.
Time 30 seconds.
Points 1 point per repetition.

Motivation

The most difficult part of any exercise plan is finding the motivation to do it in the first place. The Marines are renowned for instilling in their recruits a mental toughness that enables them to tackle serious physical challenges in real life, as well as in training. Their famous 50 mile yomp across the Falklands in 1982 – carrying packs averaging 110 lbs across mountainous, inhospitable terrain in almost continuous rain and near-freezing temperatures – demonstrated perfectly the strategic value of having troops who can not only cope with but rise above challenges and hardships that would confound many soldiers.

So, to rise above a physical challenge requires not just physical training – at some point all bodies fail their owners. You also need a determined mind that will not, cannot, countenance failure. In a Marine training troop there are always others to jolly you along, whether it be with a helping push or an acerbic tongue, which can get you through low points when you hit them. However, there comes a point when the only person that stands between you and jacking it all in is yourself.

Self-motivation is not an inherited ability. But anybody can learn how to become and stay motivated. Remember that.

Why are you reading this book? Did you buy it for yourself because you want to get fit? Or did somebody who thinks you should be fitter give it to you as a present? Why do you want to get fit? Have you tried and failed to complete exercise programmes in the past? If you failed, was there a genuine reason for failure or have you concocted an excuse? Ultimately only you can answer these questions. But if you want to reap the benefits from the Royal Marines Total Fitness Programme, you must be determined to succeed before you start.

Mind over body

Being physically fit is as much dependent on your state of mind as having a perfect body. Just like a car, if your body is properly tuned it works better. This programme has been designed to make you think just as much as when to go running. Getting fit is good for your life, your work and probably your sex life – though there's no guarantee about that! If your mind is clear, because you have worked away those

When you are dog tired, carrying 22lbs in body pouches plus an SA80 rifle that always gets in the way and with a body that doesn't always do what you tell it, tackling the nets on the Tarzan-Assault Course demands more from a Marine than just superb physical fitness. He has to really want to get up there.
Picture by Matthew Ford

cobwebs and trimmed a couple of inches off the love handles it will impress colleagues at work, your friends and family, and generally make your days run smoother.

Sometimes during Marine Officer Training, young men, fresh off three sleepless freezing nights on Dartmoor, are rudely awakened in the early hours of the morning and ordered to write essays. This is not gratuitous cruelty but intended to make them aware of how important it is to be able to think clearly in high stress conditions. The victims have no choice in this matter but you do. The most difficult part of the Royal Marines Total Fitness Programme is working the part of your body which doesn't get stretched by going for runs, and which can't be exercised by multitudes of press-ups – your brain.

Before you embark on the programme, you have to want to change and be prepared to undergo the humiliation of failing, being sneered at by family and colleagues – which, believe me, is a whole lot easier than being 'beasted' by Marine Physical Training Instructors. Marine recruits – known throughout the Corps as 'nods' – have a 30 week training course where the eventual physical goal is to pass the Commando Tests and earn their 'green lid'. Winning this beret is their motivation. What is yours? You must have something to aim at.

So, the first thing to do is to set yourself a physical goal. Not an impossible one like qualifying for the Olympic 100 metres final but something you have always whispered quietly to yourself, 'I could do that', but somehow never got around to. Maybe it is running a marathon, or a half marathon, and completing it in a reasonable time; or cycling from London to Brighton in under three hours; walking Offa's Dyke, carrying a back pack, without having to rest every ten minutes for half an hour. Choose a goal which is difficult but not impossible to achieve within a set time limit.

As training progresses you will set yourself smaller goals, but always keep the main target at the back of your mind. 'Today I will complete the 4 mile run in under 35 minutes and tomorrow I will manage another 5 press-ups with a two-year-old sitting on my back'. Don't give up hope if you fail because you will. Tell yourself things like, 'OK, so I didn't manage it this time, but I will the next'.

How to keep going

The hardest part will be carrying on after your first failure, because that is when most people abandon new exercise routines. Targets must be realistic and a challenge must be attainable.

When Marines go through their training they do so in large groups so much of their motivation comes from peer pressure and fear of public failure. This helps, certainly, but ultimately the competition is always with yourself.

Roger Black, the English 400 metre sprinter, explains what drives him on: 'There are two things in your mind when you approach a race – a sense of achievement and a fear of failure. If you have a high fear of failure and a low need for achievement you're history; a high need of achievement and a low fear of failure that's perfect. I don't race other runners, I race against myself. My intention is always to run the perfect race and I know that it is possible to come second and still win by running that perfect race. Somebody else can always run faster than you but that doesn't matter if you have achieved everything you set out to do. There is always another time.' Champion athletes know how important motivation is. Most of us tend to forget that ultimately it is the mind that wills the body on. Once you have grasped this, you are almost halfway to being at Commando Level, but remember to give your body time to catch up with your brain.

Don't forget that your brain is part of your body, not a disembodied grey jelly wobbling about behind your eyes. It is constantly sending and receiving messages – a lot more efficiently than many military radios – and triggering off chemical releases in the body. Everybody knows what an adrenalin rush feels like – there's a surge of energy into the muscles, bringing with it a feeling of power, and an increase in heart rate follows. There is a knack to channelling adrenalin, to controlling the anticipation of energy, which you can learn with practice.

A well-nourished brain can be a friend. Long distance runners often talk about 'the wall', the point at which their brain and body are, for once, in total agreement. Neither can go on and neither have any intention of doing so. However if you break through the wall, your body will get an amazing sense of well being, of euphoria, as if you are floating, not running. The brain creates chemicals called endorphins and encephalins which are painkillers – natural opiates capable of giving a natural high. However, as with morphine you also get a come down after breaking through the wall, but by that point you have already won the race with yourself and your feeling of achievement will quickly outweigh any exhaustion.

Reinforcing your self-esteem

You might have wondered why you were asked to measure various parts of your anatomy in the first chapter. The intention was not to send you spiralling into a fit of depression and self-loathing, though that can be quite a spur in its own right. It was intended to give you a yardstick

so you can gauge what changes occur in your physique over the next sixteen weeks.

Anybody who is prepared to take the Royal Marines Total Fitness Programme seriously must possess a certain amount of vanity – or, at the very least, concern – for his body. Over the course your body will change, not radically, but sufficiently to attract comments from friends and family. Don't spend too much time gazing at your reflection in the mirror, or glowering when the scales refuse to confirm that the pounds have tumbled off (muscle weighs more than fat so your weight loss may not be as great as you might expect). Instead, check your weight and measurements before you go on to the next Level of training. Then

you will be pleasantly surprised to see that flab has become muscle, that your tummy seems to have shrunk or that your shoulders seem broader.

Increased self-esteem will help to increase your ability to cope with increasing physical discomfort. At the same time, don't give in to depression if it takes longer than you thought it would to progress from Couch Potato to Commando. You cannot win a war if you aren't prepared to fight battles on the way – some of which you may lose.

Preparing for Tests

On Day 6 of every week in the training programme you are always

Down at Lympstone Commando Training Centre, when the tide recedes on the River Exe it leaves miles of black smelly mud – perfect for Marine training. The Mud Run looks worse than it really is, as once a recruit is that filthy, doing press-ups is just another exercise. The worst bit is having the frozen mud hosed off in winter.
Picture by Matthew Ford

3 3

expected to work longer and harder. In Level 1 the day's activities take 40 minutes (excluding warming up), slowly graduating up to 2½ hours in Level 5. The Tests at each Level may take a little longer still – as there are some hidden – not always pleasant – surprises at the end of each. It is important to take this time into account when planning your schedule; the final Commando Tests are not over in a minute and the only way to prepare for covering 30 miles in 8 hours is to build up your stamina and endurance ability over a period of time. However, don't be daunted by the prospect.

You might not have taken any form of test – either physical or mental – since you left school or university or took your driving test. Indeed, you might not want to start again now, but, unless you can afford the luxury of a personal trainer, the only way to measure an improvement in your physical well-being is to put it to trial. Even with a trainer, or a supervised gym programme, you are being pushed along all the time. In the Royal Marines Total Fitness Programme, the Tests are a benchmark of your personal achievement. It is you, the individual in track suit and training shoes, who is the victor, albeit of a small short-term goal.

A Marine under training has one major advantage over you in that he is being guided through a strict training curriculum and he has the cushion – though it's sometimes a bed of nails – of a group around him. Generally people perform better if they are in competition with others, yet at the highest levels it is not a question of beating another man, it is about competing with yourself. What this boils down to is that you must be in the right frame of mind and be properly prepared seriously before you take the Tests. They are not impossible but they will prove to be too physically demanding if you are not ready. Preparation is not just physical it is mental, too.

The following experience shows just how true this can be. A Jamaican on a recent Royal Marine young officer training course was desperate to earn his green beret. He was fit enough in trainers, and without webbing (a series of pouches attached to his belt) or weapon he was a fast, confident runner. Yet as soon as he pulled on his boots and was confronted with the reality of a test, something else took hold of him. Maybe it was a combination of fear and too much longing to succeed. Whatever it was, it took possession of his mind and he lost the battle before he even started it. He would breathe too fast, hyper-ventilate and lose coordination. Encouragement, even physical jollying along, by other members of his batch was counterproductive; he needed support but instead rejected it. Left to run on his own he panicked – tunnels and ropes took on a monstrous significance and by the time he had finished the Endurance Course (3 minutes over time) his face looked grey and old before its time. Yet a week earlier, accompanied by three others over the same course, he was only 30 seconds over the time limit. For him it was a case of his brain telling his body that it could not do something even though it was actually more than capable of doing it.

Now the reverse is also true. If your brain insists you can do something, your body will follow, albeit in a somewhat grudging manner, as I discovered when I went on my 30 Miler in June 1992. There was a time, for a long hour five hours in to the run, when I was alone and miserable, even beyond 'threaders' (Marine slang for exhausted). I was lagging far behind a six-man syndicate and the messages from my brain to my legs were resulting in zero response. Sure, they complied in a tired fashion. As the hairpin climb up to the final checkpoint seemed to go on for ever, I managed to scale the wall without realizing it and then the energy that had seemed lost for ever came back. The next and last leg was over a hill that has broken many hearts and spirits – it has not one but six false summits. True, I was going very slowly by this point but nothing was going to stop me finishing.

That same day two of the young officers were running the 30 Miler with injuries – under close supervision – that no civilian should run with. One had a barely mended stress fracture of the foot and the other had shin splints, so that every time his heel hit the tarmac it hurt like hell. Everybody finished within the time limit, and everybody, not just those carrying injuries or 'fat civvies', later admitted they had passed through a period where all they wanted to do was to throw their kit on the ground and give up.

The salutary moral tales are now over; they are simply to show that the primary motivation in taking any of the tests in this book will be psychological. Don't, however, be a puritan and let the Royal Marines Total Fitness Programme run your life. Stay relaxed, don't try to take the tests the morning after a night before. If this is the situation, have your rest day 24 hours early and then do it.

Check you have all the kit you need, stopwatch, trainers, bike, and so on. Make sure you are properly warmed up – that there is a thin glow of sweat on your body, and your muscles are well stretched. Before doing the Commando Tests, the Marines will warm up for 20 minutes, while athletes may take 45–60 minutes prior to a race. Walk around for a minute or so, thinking about what you have to do. Then do it. But first, after doing the Initial Fitness Test, before you can move on to any Level, you have to survive J Week.

J Week

When a Marine recruit joins up, his first week is known as 'J Week' – or Joining Week. Compared to what he will endure in the following 29 weeks of training it is a doddle, but it is essential because a high intensity training programme must be approached gently and with respect. As the military axiom goes: time spent on reconnaissance is seldom wasted. J Week is packed with advice and is, if you like, a seven day learning experience.

Anyone who has taken the IFT and is preparing to go on to any of the first three Levels needs an extra week just to get into the swing of things – to prepare to take some exercise every day perhaps for the first time in years. It is important to be relaxed, and to reorganize your life, clearing aside enough time for exercise in the day. Later on, as the schedule increases, it will demand even more physical and temporal commitment. Get into a good routine as soon as you can. This is not just military bullying; soon you should be happy to make the time because you can feel the benefits you are getting.

Throughout J Week, monitor your waking and resting pulse rates (see below) so you become used to the routine. Pay particular attention to taking any exercise if you are feeling under the weather – or if your pulse rate indicates you are. There is nothing worse than doing physical exercise with a mild case of flu. Physically and psychologically it could put you back weeks.

Getting to Know Your Pulse Rates

Monitoring the intensity of the exercise you take is essential for both your personal safety and the effectiveness of the Royal Marines Total Fitness Programme, or indeed any aerobic exercise programme. The body should be exercised at the appropriate intensity in order to improve cardiovascular fitness and also to avoid overfatigue which could be dangerous.

To help monitor your level of fitness, you should be aware of four pulse rates. J Week is the perfect opportunity to learn how to keep a record.

Your pulse may be found either at the main artery on the side of your neck, just below the end of your jaw, or on the flat side of your wrist in line

During J Week a young Marine gets issued with so much kit he doesn't know what to do with it. It gets much worse on his first foray out into the field - he has to fit most of it into a Bergen that suddenly becomes very small. And when he takes it out for inspection he somehow never manages to get it all in again.
Picture by Matthew Ford

with your thumb. Simply press with the first two fingers of one hand and count the number of beats. It is most accurate to take your pulse over a full minute though if rushed you can take it for 30 seconds and double it, for 15 seconds and multiply by 4, or even for 10 seconds and multiply by 6, if you are really pushed for time.

Resting pulse rate

When you wake in the morning after a good night's sleep, take your pulse rate for a minute. Do this for three days and take the average as your resting rate. In future, if the rate is over 10 beats per minute higher than your average, do not train during the day. Your pulse rate indicates that you are too tired and have not recovered fully from the previous day's exertions.

Working pulse rate

Check your pulse rate after a normal morning's activity at work. On average, it should be about 10 beats per minute higher than your resting rate. If your rate is too high on waking but returns to normal during the day, then you can consider training again that day.

Maximum heart rate

For a simple guideline deduct your age in years from 220. This is your maximum heart rate (MHR) – the maximum amount your heart can beat in a minute. If your pulse rate is above this, you are pushing yourself too hard and depriving your blood of oxygen. Exercising in an 'anaerobic' state (without enough oxygen) can only be for a short period; you run the risk of injury if you continue for too long.

Target heart rate zone

Your aim is to get your pulse rate up to 60–85 per cent of your MHR. However, to begin with you should not work at levels above 75 per cent MHR. If you do not achieve this rate for more than 20 minutes at least three times a week, you are not actually increasing your training capability – merely standing still.

Monitoring your pulse rate regularly is an extremely effective indication of how fit you are becoming. The pulse rate of an adult man, awake but at rest, can vary from 60–80 beats per minute but is on average 70–72 beats per minute (a woman's average rate is slightly higher at 78–82).

Before I started exercising my waking pulse rate was usually 60–62, giving a working rate of 70–72 (spot on the national average). By the time I took the Commando Test six months later it was 52–54 on waking after a good sleep and a 60–62 working rate. When I visited an acupuncturist for treatment on a knee problem, I was most gratified to be told: 'We don't hear many pulse rates this low in a man of your age.'

J Week Routine

Before moving on to the J Week programme make sure you understand the importance of warming up, stretching and warming down. It will save you a great deal of unnecessary pain in the weeks to come.
Warming up
　　You should never undertake any strenuous physical activity without making sure that your whole body is warmed up. Trying to run from a cold start – especially on a winter's morning – multiplies the chances of inflicting injury.

　　The Royal Marines Total Fitness Programme will prepare you gradually and thoroughly for the final Test week. However, any form of physical activity involves an element of risk from injury, most of which come in the form of minor strains and sprains. The risk of injury to muscles and tendons can be effectively and substantially reduced by regularly warming up, stretching and warming down the major muscles of the body.

Tips on warming up

Although you may be keen to get on with your training, if you adopt the right attitude to warming up, everything will go more smoothly. Remember the following:

● Warm ups should be seen as an essential part of the activity – not an unnecessary extra.
● A warm body will perform better.
● A warm body is less likely to attract niggling injuries.
● Time spent warming up is never wasted.
● Warm up in the environment in which you are going to exercise (inside for the circuit, outside for running, yomping and cycling).

The aim of a warm-up is to prepare the body for more strenuous exercise to come. Initially you should aim to follow this four part routine – Light mobility exercises, Initial warm-up, Stretching and Final warm-up – until it is second nature to you before taking any physical exercise.

Light mobility exercises

Take a couple of minutes to loosen the joints of the body. The purpose of these simple exercises (see pages 42–47) is to get synovial fluid secreted into the joints. The fluid acts as a lubricant, enabling the joints to function smoothly and thereby preventing injury. Continue with each exercise until you feel a sensation in the area of the body being worked.

Initial Warm-up

Spend 5 minutes on a light warm-up consisting of jogging or skipping. Make large body movements, swinging your arms and legs to increase and stimulate the flow of blood to all the working muscles. This should increase your body temperature and pulse rate, and put a glow or thin sheen of sweat on your skin.

Stretching

It is advisable to perform these stretches (see pages 48–57) at least ONCE a day. And for the exercises to be of proper benefit, you must stretch CORRECTLY. Make a habit of stretching all the major muscle groups for a total of up to 10 minutes every day. Work from the top of the body downwards – and always do the stretches in the sequence illustrated.

TEN GOLDEN RULES

1 Ensure you are in the correct start position.
2 Breathe naturally. NEVER hold your breath – a common mistake.
3 Always stretch and release the stretch SLOWLY.
4 Keep your joints in alignment.
5 NEVER bounce – this causes an unnatural elasticity in the muscles and leads to injury.
6 NEVER ask a friend to push the stretch further – this is a specialized form of stretching.
7 Hold each stretch for 6–10 second for upper body muscles and 20–30 seconds for lower body and legs.
8 Relax under control.
9 Stretch each muscle group only once per stretching session.
10 Take a Whole Body Approach – stretching all the major muscle groups – and work from the top of the body downwards.

If the day's schedule includes running, cycling or yomping (load carrying), concentrate on stretching your legs by holding those stretches for the maximum (30 seconds).

4 Final Warm-up

After stretching you should do a more rigorous warm-up for 3–5 minutes. Start with some running, skipping and jumping. Follow up with light circuit exercises: Sit-ups × 2 repetitions; Press-ups × 2 repetitions; Squat Thrusts × 2 repetitions and Dips × 2 repetitions (see pages 24–27). At this point you should be sweating and be physically and mentally prepared for the exercise to come.

Keep the Whole Body Approach in mind, so if, for example, the day's activity is to be a circuit this second warm-up should be quite hard. If you are going to cycle, concentrate on the legs. If you will be yomping, concentrate on the legs, torso and shoulders (they take the weight of the pack). If you are swimming, warm up the whole body.

Perhaps surprisingly, an unfit person will warm up much faster than a fit one. The fitter you get the longer the second warm-up will take to work. If for some reason time is at a premium, miss out on the initial warm-up and just do the light mobility exercises, stretching exercises and final warm-up in that order.

Warming Down

In the same way that warming up and stretching correctly are vital, it is essential to know how to warm down after any exercise.

Tips on warming down
- Calm down slowly and gradually.
- Don't just stop.
- Always stretch, even if it's a short one. Make this a habit.

Warming down should consist of a warm-down phase and another stretching session. Start with easy but large, swinging body movements, easing down to small movements. Begin by jogging with both arms swinging, then just a jog, then slow down to a walking jog, then a side step until you come to a natural halt. Never stop suddenly. The aim is to bring the heart rate down slowly – warming down correctly will also delay the onset of muscle strain.

Try to calm down slowly then stretch the major muscle groups again (remembering the Whole Body Approach). Spend 6–10 seconds on upper body muscles and 20–30 seconds on lower body and legs.

REMEMBER: If you don't warm up and stretch before exercise and warm down afterwards you increase the risk of injury. Then there will only be one person to blame – and you know who it is!

LIGHT MOBILITY EXERCISES
Arm Circles

● Stand with feet hip-width apart, knees slightly bent. With both arms fully extended, swing the arms around in large sweeping circles.
● Repeat arm circles in each direction.

LIGHT MOBILITY EXERCISES

Hip and Trunk Rotation

● Stand with feet hip-width apart, knees slightly bent, hands on hips.
  Without moving the lower body, rotate the torso and hips, taking them
  to the right, to the back, to the left and to the front again.
● Repeat rotations in each direction.

LIGHT MOBILITY EXERCISES
Knee Bends

- Stand with feet hip-width apart, knees bent and hands placed on knees.
- Keeping your hands on your knees, flex the knees up and down. Do not let your bottom go lower than the level of your knees and keep your knees bent throughout.
- Repeat.

LIGHT MOBILITY EXERCISES
Ankle Rotations

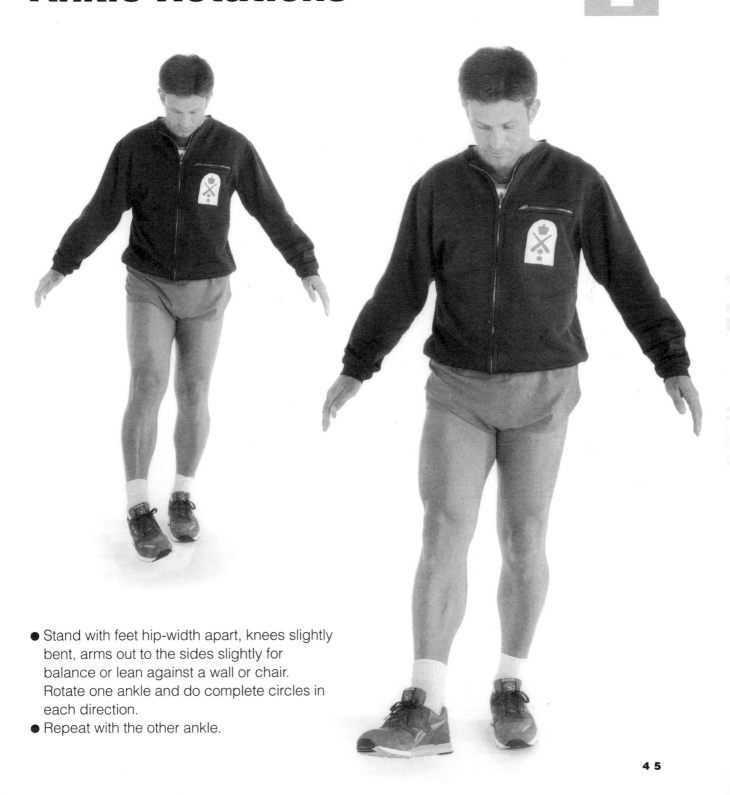

- Stand with feet hip-width apart, knees slightly bent, arms out to the sides slightly for balance or lean against a wall or chair. Rotate one ankle and do complete circles in each direction.
- Repeat with the other ankle.

LIGHT MOBILITY EXERCISES
Forward Bends

- Stand with feet hip-width apart, knees slightly bent, hands on hips.
- Bend forwards from the hips and then back up to the vertical position. Do not lean backwards when coming back up.
- Repeat.

LIGHT MOBILITY EXERCISES

Neck Loosener

- Stand with feet hip-width apart, knees slightly bent, hands by your sides. Turn your head to look over your right shoulder.
- Turn your head to the front and then over to your left shoulder.
- Repeat.

- When you have completed your repetitions take your chin down to rest on your chest. Bring your chin back up to the centre. Never take your head backwards.
- Repeat.

STRETCHING EXERCISES
Tricep Stretch

- Stand with feet hip-width apart, knees slightly bent. Place the palm of your right hand flat between your shoulder blades, elbow pointing upwards, and bring your left arm over your head and place the hand on top of your right elbow. Push down with your left hand on to your right elbow and hold for 6–10 seconds. Do not push too far. Keep your shoulders pulled back.
- Swap arms and repeat.

STRETCHING EXERCISES

Shoulder Stretch

- Stand with feet shoulder-width apart, knees slightly bent. Place your right arm across your chest and bring your left arm up, bent, to hold your right elbow against your chest.
- Pull your left forearm towards your body, pressing on the right elbow and hold for 6–10 seconds.
- Swap arms and repeat.

STRETCHING EXERCISES

Upper Back Stretch

● Stand with feet hip-width apart, knees slightly bent. Extend your arms out in front, level with your shoulders, hands clasped and palms facing outwards (do not interlock fingers). Push forwards with hands and hold for 6–10 seconds.

STRETCHING EXERCISES
Chest Stretch

● Stand with feet hip-width apart, knees slightly
bent and hands clasped together behind
your back (do not interlock fingers).
Raise your arms as high as you can behind
you and hold for 6–10 seconds.

STRETCHING EXERCISES
Side Stretch

- Stand with feet 18–24 inches apart, knees slightly bent. Place your left hand on your thigh and reach up with your right arm. Lean over to the left and hold for 6–10 seconds. Do not lean forwards or backwards and do not lock the knees.
- Swap arms and repeat to the other side.

STRETCHING EXERCISES
Stomach and Back Stretch

- Kneel on all fours with knees apart for balance and hands shoulder-width apart. Round your back up, like a cat, and hold for 20–30 seconds.
- Slowly release and arch your back, pushing your stomach down towards floor. Hold for 20–30 seconds.

STRETCHING EXERCISES
Quad Stretch

- Stand and hold on to the back of a chair for support. Take hold of your right foot at the instep and pull the heel towards your bottom. Try to keep the knees touching. Hold for 20–30 seconds.
- Slowly release and repeat on the other side.

STRETCHING EXERCISES
Groin Stretch

● Sit with the soles of your feet together and hold on to your legs just above the ankles, with elbows placed on the inside of your knees.
● Use your elbows to push your knees down towards the floor. Hold for 20–30 seconds.

STRETCHING EXERCISES
Hamstring Stretch

- Lie on your back with your head resting on the floor, with one knee bent and foot flat on the floor. Bend the other knee in towards your chest and take hold of the calf with both hands. Slowly pull the lower part of your leg towards you trying to straighten it as much as possible and hold for 20–30 seconds.
- Slowly release leg, place the foot flat on the floor and repeat with the other leg.

STRETCHING EXERCISES
Calf Stretch

● Stand with feet hip-width apart, one foot placed in front of the other and hands placed on your hips. Both feet should be parallel. Keeping the back heel on the floor, slowly bend the front knee and hold for 20–30 seconds. Keep the front knee over the ankle.

● Slowly release and repeat with the other leg in front.

J Week: Day 1 Draw kit

In other words, and civvy speak, check the equipment you will need for the next 16 weeks.

It is really unnecessary to rush out and spend a fortune on new equipment. You will probably have already acquired over the years much of what you need. Before I started my training I had a mountain bike, an old battered day sack, a pair of walking boots and various T-shirts and sweat pants of varying colours and origins. These lasted for weeks.

Wherever possible, beg, borrow or steal off friends until you are certain you will continue to use the gear. The same goes for joining a local gym or health club. Most make their profit from people who have a fit of fitness guilt, join up, go a few times and then gradually lose interest and enthusiasm. In a strange way spending a lot of money on kit initially may work against you, building up a subconscious resentment.

You will need:

1 Good walking boots, with thick rubber soles, giving high ankle support and waterproof uppers. Military issue boots are adequate once they are worn in, but there are plenty of lighter boots available which over long distances will be worth their weight in gold and blister free recovery. Gore-tex uppers are excellent, until you actually step into a puddle deeper than the boot – then it is as hard for water to get out as it usually is to get in!

2 Training/running shoes. If you need to buy a pair, go along to a local athletics store that knows its business, for advice. Take an old pair of trainers with you. An assistant should ask you the following questions:
- How heavy are you?
- What is your running style? Do you run with the weight on the outside or the inside of the foot? Does your heel or toe strike most heavily? You should be able to tell this from looking at the old pair of trainers, or the shop assistant should know from allowing you to run around the block a couple of times – if you can persuade him or her to let you try them out before you buy.
- How many miles a week are you intending to cover and on what terrain – tarmac, path, cross country or whatever? If you are running primarily on roads, invest in shoes with the maximum cushioning.
- How much do you want to spend? Answer this after everything else. The golden rule is do not try to economize. However, some of the most expensive running shoes may simply not be suited for your style. I bought a pair of cheap and cheerful running shoes and within 6 weeks

I had knees that alternated between jelly and gravel grating on bone. The Marine recruits are issued with Reebok Phase 4 trainers but for around £50 you should be able to find the right shoes.

3 Access to a bicycle. A static exercise bike will do initially but in the long term it is a cop out as it will not allow for changes in terrain, climatic conditions and so on. Most gyms and health clubs now have sophisticated computer-programmed bikes, so explain to the assistant what you want to do. Mountain bikes, which have wider tyres and tougher frames, are generally better for coping with big city potholes than racing bikes – but they are heavier to ride. For size the bike frame should be 10 inches shorter than your inside leg measurement.

4 Beg, borrow or steal a small day pack. For comfort it should have both a waist and chest strap and be capable of carrying the emergency kit listed below. This is the minimum you should take with you for safety if you are going cross country. If you are walking around town, it is good practice to wear it so you get used to carrying weight.

- Waterproof clothes. As with boots, Gore-tex are best because they allow moisture to escape. Nylon waterproofs trap your own body moisture inside and you can end up just as sweaty and damp as you would if you stood in the rain.
- Flask with hot or cold drink – depending on your preference and/or the weather.
- Bag of sweets of your choice – boiled sweets and chocolate bars are recommended.
- Basic training clothes: vest, shorts, a track suit (shell suits are definitely out and sweat bottoms can be too heavy if they get wet), sport socks.

5 Optional: Woolly hat and gloves for winter, fluorescent vest and reflective ankle bands for running on dark mornings or evenings.

After checking your kit, familiarize yourself with all the stretching exercises until you are comfortable with the movements. Stretching should become second nature. Make stretching a habit, not a chore. If you find yourself waiting in a queue, stretch your arms and legs; the more flexible you are, the faster your recovery time will be.
Have you monitored your pulse rate today?

Day 2 Check your route

Start with a full warm-up and stretching session (see pages 39–57). Get a little glow on, then walk and jog gently on a recce around your chosen running route of around 2 miles. Try to choose one where there isn't too much traffic or too many roads to cross. Also plan the route so that it can be extended further as the training progresses.

Warm down (page 41).

Have you monitored your pulse rate today?

Day 3 Introduction to Individual Circuit

Circuit Testing

The circuits are the core exercises for the training programme. They have been drawn up so that they can be done by individuals in an enclosed space – like on board ship, or in a hotel room – and they require no specialist equipment. Even at the Commando Level, with a proper stretching and warm-up routine all the circuit exercises can be completed within a half hour period – at the end of which you will know you've taken some exercise.

Therefore it is very important that you learn how to set up your circuit routine correctly. In each Level (except Level 1) there will be two Circuit days. One is a free choice of a number of exercises with a varying number of repetitions. The second is the Individual Circuit, which has to be completed within a specific target time before you can move on to the next Level. Each exercise is designed to tone up either the Arms, Legs or Torso and will be marked (A), (L) or (T) accordingly, and occasionally I have included a general exercise (G). Obviously it takes time to get into the rhythm of doing different exercises. Some, like the dreaded Crunchies (my personal *bête noire*) and V-sits, are initially hard to coordinate.

The essence of the circuit lies in testing and re-testing each exercise at each Level. It is always better to have someone else do the testing. Such attention to detail is not just a slavish following of the rules. If you get the fundamentals of an exercise wrong at the beginning, it can be very hard to correct later and in extreme cases – as you push yourself harder – it might lead to niggling injuries, pulled muscles and the like. Ultimately, of course, cutting corners is a personal choice. Everyone does it, even if they are unaware of it, and they may never be found out. As luck will have it, though, people tend to be found out when it matters most – hitting the wall halfway across Dartmoor, or in a marathon, and not being able to climb over it. So if you cheat – and you will – the only person being cheated is yourself.

It is easy to test for the circuits. First you need to make a photocopy of the circuit sheet (see page 65) or draw your own version. Warm up with a 10 minute gentle paced jog (just enough to get a bit of sweat going) and some stretching. Before testing make sure you have mastered the relevant exercise, maybe even running through it a couple of times to make sure you have it right.

Testing

Check which exercises you have to do for the Level you are at. Don't forget you need a stopwatch and preferably someone timing you.

1 Note down the exercises for your relevant level on the sheet in the order you will carry them out.

2 In 30 seconds do as many repetitions of the first exercise as you can. Make a note of the number you do on the sheet.

3 Take a minute's breather.

4 Repeat the process with each exercise until you have completed all the ones for your Level.

5 Divide the number of repetitions in half. If you have an odd number take the lower figure. Later on you will be very grateful for such small mercies!

6 Now do the circuit twice (or three times depending on Level) as fast as you can, timing the end result. You calculate your target time as two thirds of the time you achieved on your first completed circuit.

Example After testing in Level 1 you might have a circuit sheet that looks like this:

Exercise	Test Repetitions	Circuit Repetitions
Half sit-ups	21	10
Dips	19	9
Step-ups	16	8
Dorsal Raises	12	6
Time taken = 4 minutes		
Target time = 2 minutes 40 seconds		

7 Walk around for a minute or so. Do a proper warm-down and stretching routine.

Now cheer up. That target time will be achieved much quicker than you think. Familiarity with the exercises will speed the repetitions.

NOTE: You will follow this same procedure when you re-test your Individual Circuit at each new Level.

Try to perform your circuits in a warm airy room with plenty of light. During the summer months I always preferred to do them in the garden on a mat. You will find that congenial surroundings work wonders if you are exercising alone.

Did you warm up and stretch first?

Have you monitored your pulse rate today?

Day 4

Recce bike route – if possible add some hills, don't stick to the flat.

Did you warm up and stretch first?

Have you monitored your pulse rate today?

Day 5

Jog that 20 minute route again.

Did you warm up and stretch first?

Have you monitored your pulse rate today?

Day 6

Recce load carry route. Check that your pack fits, doesn't rub, and that your walking boots also fit comfortably.

Then go to your local swimming pool and swim 250 metres (10 lengths of 25 metres each or the equivalent). Breaststroke exercises the whole body better than crawl – which is better for speed and stamina. For the best mix you should alternate strokes every two lengths. Backstroke and butterfly – probably the most difficult stroke ever invented – are optional. There may be some of you who want to carry out the Royal Marines Total Fitness Programme but have never learnt to swim. Unfortunately the problem is that there is no really acceptable substitute. Swimming is one of the most efficient and effective forms of exercise because the water itself is a tremendous aid to the body.

Because swimming is a non weight-bearing exercise, it leads to good aerobic conditioning without any of the risk of injury that can bedevil athletes who train exclusively on terra firma.

If you want to imitate the beneficial effects of swimming as closely as possible without swimming, you could try these alternatives:

1 **Upper body circuit** Choose from the upper body circuit exercises in this book and do them in an arm, torso sequence. Make sure you perform them as quickly as possible because the emphasis is on endurance. This will simulate the action of swimming, in terms of speed and movement. The time taken on each set of exercises should be as close to the time it would take to swim one 50 metre length in a pool. For example, if you were to spend 15 seconds per exercise on a sequence of press-ups, sit-ups, dips and dorsals, this would be the equivalent of swimming one 50 metre length in 1 minute.

2 **Elastics** This equipment can be either bought or made. The ones you can buy are approximately 4 metres long with a hand strap at each end. The elastic is looped through a bar or similar inanimate object at a height of about 1 metre. The elastic is then stretched to a level relative to the person's strength so that all the main swimming motions of front crawl can be simulated. The best use of elastics is Interval Training (i.e. 1 minute's work, 1 minute's rest etc). The intervals can be adapted to suit the individual's strength and ability.

Elastics can be made out of inner tubes for bicycles or any piece of strong rubber tubing.

3 **Swim benches** Some health clubs and sports' centres have specialized benches that you lie on, and by using elastic cords, you simulate the motions of swimming.

4 **Wet vests** These do not simulate swimming but are, none the less, excellent buoyancy aids that enable a person to run in the water while remaining afloat in the upright position. Generally used for remedial work, once you have mastered them they can provide an excellent workout. They can be bought at most large sports' stores or via mail order swim catalogues.

If you are a poor swimmer, remember that one of the final Commando Tests is a 500 metre swim in under 10 minutes. So if you are determined to follow the programme properly, your only option is to take up the challenge and become a stronger swimmer.

The Royal Marines Total Fitness Programme would not be complete without yomping. The yomp is one of the major *raison d'êtres* for the

Marine Corps – the ability to travel across the most inhospitable terrain, while carrying all you need for survival, and still being capable of fighting at the other end. Marching in boots is a specialized specific skill which no Marine can be without. Obviously if you live and train in a major urban area, the prospect of walking for miles over roads, past buildings punctuated with the odd piece of greenery may not be appealing. However, if you can structure your training week so that the Load Carry/Yomp is on a weekend it can easily become the most favoured part of training and one that your friends, family and dogs can actually join in.

Although you might feel an idiot when you first start walking in boots with a heavy pack, you do get used to it very quickly. Incidentally it's also excellent training for anybody who wants to go on long walks with babies or toddlers in slings or carry frames who, when asleep, have a dead weight that makes an 80 lb pack seem light! Unfortunately there is no real equivalent in training to carrying a pack in boots other than carrying a light pack, wearing your boots in and slowly increasing the weights in the pack until you are ready to tackle the Load Carry and the 30 Miler. If, for assorted personal reasons, you simply do not want to train for those specific tests after you have reached Level 3, see page 121 for an alternative training programme.

Did you warm up and stretch first?
Have you monitored your pulse rate today?

Day 7 Rest

A rest day can often be more important in training than a day of exercise. It is essential to give your body a chance to recover, particularly if you are unaccustomed to taking physical exercise. You are bound to have minor aches and pains but a slight niggle can easily get worse if you don't give it a chance to recover.

Have you monitored your pulse rate today?
Now stop and consider. Are you ready to move on to the first week?

If you are not comfortable or convinced, this is a chance to opt out and do another week of gentle warm-ups. In the Marines, recruits who are not performing up to the expected physical standards get 'back trooped'. Throughout this book if you fail the tests required to move up a Level you will be 'back trooped' until you can pass the test. The onus is on you.

Your Circuit Sheet

Exercise	Test Reps	Circuit Reps	Time Taken	Target Time	
Half Sit-Ups (T)					**LEVEL 1**
Dips (A)					
Step-Ups (L)					
Dorsal Raises (G)					
Press-Ups (A)					**LEVEL 2**
Squats (L)					
Sit-Ups (T)					**LEVEL 3**
Wide-Arm Press-Ups (A)					
Alternate Leg Squat Thrusts (L)					
Sit-Ups with a Twist (T)					**LEVEL 4**
Dorsals (G)					
Squat Thrusts (G)					
V-Sits (T)					
Clap Press-Ups (A)					**LEVEL 5**
Tuck Jumps (L)					
Crunchies (T)					

CIRCUIT EXERCISES
Half Sit-Ups (T)

- Lie flat on your back with knees bent, hands placed on thighs.
- Sit up so that your hands touch your kneecaps, but keep your lower back on the floor.
- Return to the starting position and repeat.

CIRCUIT EXERCISES
Dips (A)

● Sit on the edge of a chair, hands facing forwards and resting on the edge of the seat. Keeping your knees bent and feet flat on the floor, move your torso and knees forwards, so that your bottom comes off the chair and your weight is supported on your hands.

● Using the strength of your arms to support you, flex your elbows so that your bottom is lowered towards, but does not touch, the floor. Straighten your arms (but do not lock them) to raise yourself up again.
● Repeat.

CIRCUIT EXERCISES

Step-Ups (L)

- Stand in front of a 12-inch high platform or bench.
- Start with your right foot and step up on to the platform.
- Step up with your left foot. Step back off the platform with your right foot first, following with your left foot.
- Repeat, this time stepping up with your left foot first. When you step up, always straighten the leg. The heels must always make contact with the platform.
- Repeat step-ups, leading with alternate feet.

CIRCUIT EXERCISES
Dorsal Raises (G)

This is a general back exercise which also stretches the stomach muscles. It is a particularly useful exercise to practise after doing sit-ups.

● Lie flat on your stomach with your forehead on the floor, arms bent, hands shoulder-width apart, palms flat on floor and facing forwards.

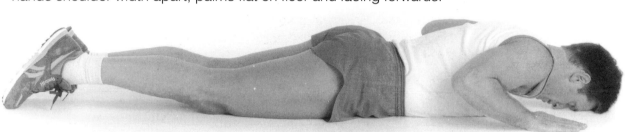

● Straighten your arms and use the strength of your back to raise your torso off the floor. Keep your hips on the floor throughout.
● Return to the starting position and repeat.

CIRCUIT EXERCISES
Press-Ups (A)

- Start face down, hands shoulder-width apart, legs and body straight, your head in line with your body. Only the palms of the hands and the balls of the feet touch the floor.
- Keeping your back straight, bend your arms and lower your chest to the floor. Straighten your arms (but do not lock them) and raise the chest to return to the starting position.
- Repeat, making sure that the chest touches the floor with each repetition.

- If at first you are not strong enough to do the full press-ups, you can keep the knees on the floor during this exercise until you have built up more strength in your arms.

CIRCUIT EXERCISES
Squats (L)

- Stand with both heels raised on a plank of wood no more than 2 inches (but not less than 1½ inches) thick. This helps you to keep your balance during the exercise.
- Bend your knees, making sure that your bottom does not go lower than the level of your knees. Straighten your knees slightly but do not come all the way up.
- Repeat.

CIRCUIT EXERCISES

Sit-Ups (T)

● Lie on your back with your hands placed across your chest, knees bent, feet hip-width apart and flat on the floor. (You may hook your feet under a chair or bar if necessary.)
● Raise your upper body into a sitting position.
● Return to the starting position and repeat.

CIRCUIT EXERCISES
Wide-Arm Press-Ups (A)

- Proceed as for standard press-ups (see Level 2) but with arms placed wider apart.
- Lower and raise the chest as before, making sure that the chest touches the floor with each repetition. During the lowered position the palms should be directly under the elbows.

CIRCUIT EXERCISES
Alternate Leg Squat Thrusts (L)

- Start in the standard press-ups position (with arms below shoulders) legs outstretched behind.
- Thrust your right leg forwards until the knee is through the arms.

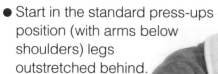

- Bring your right leg back and thrust your left leg forwards.
- Repeat, thrusting alternate legs forwards. Keep on the balls of your feet throughout.

CIRCUIT EXERCISES

Sit-Ups with a Twist (T)

- Lie on your back with knees bent, heels flat on floor, hands on temples, elbows out to the sides.
- Sit up, bringing your left elbow to touch the outside of your right knee and return to the starting position.
- Repeat with right elbow to left knee.

Dorsals (G)

This is a good general exercise for increasing overall flexibility and strengthening the lower back.

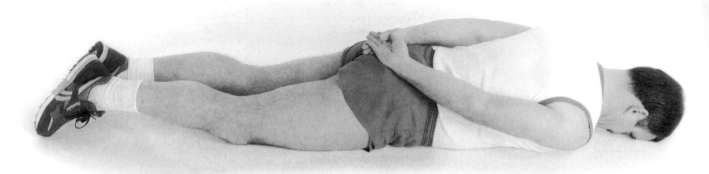

- Lie on your stomach with your forehead on the floor and hands clasped behind your back.

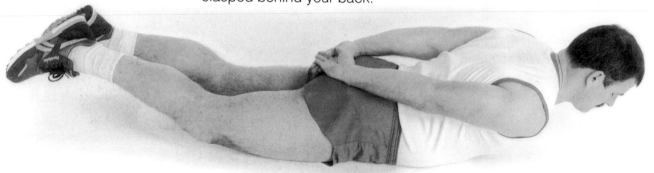

- Keeping your legs straight, lift your head, shoulders, legs (including the thighs) and chest off the floor as high as you can.
- Return to the starting position and repeat.

CIRCUIT EXERCISES
Squat Thrusts (G)

● Lie face down in the standard press-ups position (arms below shoulders), legs outstretched behind.

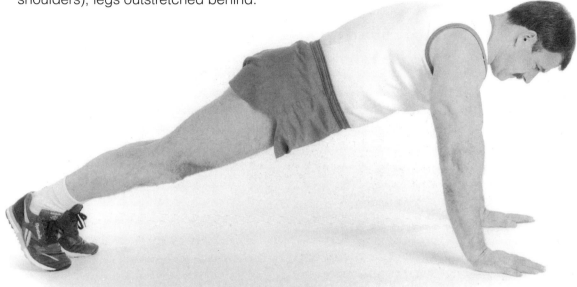

● Thrust both legs forwards so your knees are in line with your elbows. Bring both legs back to the starting position and repeat.

CIRCUIT EXERCISES
V-Sits (T)

- Lie on your back, bend both knees into your chest and raise your legs, straightening them slightly. Place your hands on your knees, your arms straight.
- Raise your head and shoulders off the floor, taking your hands off your knees and aiming your hands towards your feet. Return to the floor, placing your hands back on your knees and repeat.

CIRCUIT EXERCISES

Clap Press-Ups (A)

This is a big, explosive movement. When you first start to practise this exercise, always use a mat to cushion yourself.

- Start in the standard press-ups position.
- Lower your chest towards, but do not touch, the floor.

- Push up off the floor and clap hands before returning to the floor with arms bent.
- Raise your chest back to the starting position so that your arms are once again straight, and repeat. Try to keep the body straight during the entire movement and make the clap loud enough to be heard.

CIRCUIT EXERCISES

Tuck Jumps (L)

● Stand with feet hip-width apart, knees slightly bent.
● Jump as high as you can, aiming your knees up towards your chest. Do not bring your chest down to meet your knees.
● Repeat. Always make sure you bend the knees on landing. Never land on straight legs.

CIRCUIT EXERCISES

Crunchies (T)

● Lie flat on your back with knees bent, feet flat on the floor, hands
placed on temples, elbows out to the sides.

● Raise your bent legs and your trunk off the floor, aiming your head
towards your knees.
● Return to the starting position and repeat.

WEEKS 1–3

Couch Potato

This is it, J Week's over and you have started for real. Perhaps all you can see ahead is months of sweat and pain. Hold it. Take a deep breath. Now, forget about such negative thoughts. Instead, summon up the competitive instinct that made you get off the couch and into trainers in the first place. The very fact that you are prepared to do this means you are no longer a couch potato. Doubtless you have talked about this with friends, and maybe talked one into doing it with you. Make a serious bet with a cynical, doubting pal as to how far you will get – or both get if he's into it, too. The prospect of losing even the smallest sum of money can spur a flagging body on to almost superhuman effect.

A young Marine contemplates his future after spending the best part of a day digging himself a trench. Pausing for breath, he cannot help wondering whether he would have been better at home sitting on the couch eating chips and drinking beer while watching a war film.

Day 1: Warm up. Stretch. 20 minute run – initially you may need to walk some of the way, don't be discouraged. Warm down.

Day 2: Warm up. Stretch. Individual Circuit. In J Week you will have set your target time. Aim for target time. Warm down.

Day 3: Warm up. Stretch. 2 mile Yomp. Warm down.

Day 4: Warm up. Stretch. Swim (250 metres). If necessary, rest between lengths.

Day 5: Warm up. Stretch. 40 minute cycle ride (except for Week 3 when Individual Circuit must be completed within target time).

Day 6: Warm up. Stretch. 20 minute run and 20 minute cycle ride.

Day 7: Rest.

Notes:

Run: At this stage, you should be aiming for 10 minute miles (6 mph).

Yomp: The Marines aim consistently at a 20 minute mile (3 mph). The average person walks at 3–4 mph without kit; you'll find that after a while carrying your pack will become second nature.

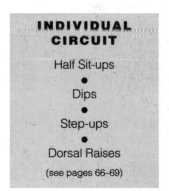

INDIVIDUAL CIRCUIT

Half Sit-ups
•
Dips
•
Step-ups
•
Dorsal Raises

(see pages 66–69)

LEVEL 1

Swim: Swim for a total of 250 metres – if you don't know the length of the pool ask the attendants. A 20 yard pool is just over 18 metres (14 lengths), 25 yards just under 23 metres (11 lengths).

Motivation Tips

- Don't exercise within an hour of eating a heavy meal, similarly don't go to sleep. Sumo wrestlers put on their massive bulk by sleeping immediately after a heavy meal.
- Some people like listening to music while exercising. If this works for you, fine, but remember that the music will directly affect the rhythm of your exercises. Up tempo aerobics favourites are better than a compilation of smouldering ballads which will slow you down and may prove distracting. If you are running with a Walkman be very careful and look out for cars, dogs and other people as you won't hear them. Never wear a Walkman when on a bike.
- If you have only estimated distances until now, borrow a pedometer, or a bike with a mileometer and measure the actual distance you run. It will invariably be less than you think.
- Wrestle with your kids. If they win perhaps you'd better stay on Level 1 another week!
- Be a narcissist. Take some pictures of yourself before you start, and keep them somewhere safe so you can compare your progress as you get fitter.
- Circuit training is designed to stress the heart and lungs. You should experience some discomfort towards the end of the circuit. However, **if you experience any sharp pain stop immediately.**
- Consider making changes to your diet by eating more carbohydrates – especially pasta, which is a good 'fuel' food. See pages 115–119 for more information.

Test

Tests should usually be carried out on Day 6 of the third week in each Level. Before taking the Test the Individual Circuit must already have been completed in target time. In Level 1, when there is only one circuit day per week, this should be done on Day 5, Week 3.

The Test has three parts:

1 A 2 mile run to be completed in under 19 minutes.

2 A 20 minute cycle ride covering not less than 5 miles.

3 10 Burpees (see opposite). These must be done correctly – no short cuts and no cheating. For every incomplete one do 2 more.

TEST EXERCISE
Burpees

- Stand erect with feet together, hands by your sides.
- Go down into the squat position, resting on the balls of your feet, with knees bent, arms straight and placed on the inside of your knees, hands flat on the floor with palms facing forwards.

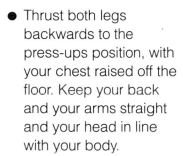

- Thrust both legs backwards to the press-ups position, with your chest raised off the floor. Keep your back and your arms straight and your head in line with your body.

- Thrust both legs forwards and return to the squat position.
- Return to the starting position and stand erect.
- Repeat the whole exercise. Always make sure you return to the full standing position between each repetition.

Civvy

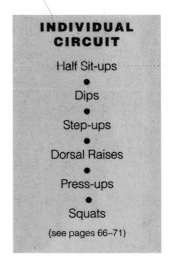

Before a Marine can fully shed his Civvy tag he must pass Initial Military Fitness – press-ups and many other exercises in perfect synchronization with the rest of his troop, while being bellowed at by an instructor. Not surprisingly, Marines hate IMF.
Picture by Robin Eggar

Congratulations! You have now become a Civvy. Come on, admit it – it wasn't half as bad as you thought it might be. The once terrifying concept of taking exercise nearly every day should now seem rather fun. So try introducing some extra exercise into your daily routine. Wherever possible walk, jog or cycle to work and when there don't take the lift – always use the stairs.

As a reward for joining Level 2 you now have an extra day of circuit training, to add to the circuit exercises for Level 1. The free choice circuit is designed not only to familiarize you with the exercises but also to work the specific muscle groups. You are free to choose 6 different exercises – 2 from each category – (see pages 66–81). They do not have to be the same exercises as you have to do in your Individual Circuit. You may consider this a good opportunity to learn the exercises for Level 3, but if you are ambitious and go for Level 5 exercises, press-ups with a clap for instance, do not expect any sympathy if you fall flat on your face!

Day 1: Warm up. Stretch. 30 minute run.
Day 2: Warm up. Stretch. Free choice circuits, choose 6 exercises (2 for arms, 2 for torso, 2 for legs – see pages 66–81), 10 repetitions of each. Rest for 1 minute. Then do another 10 repetitions of each.
Day 3: Warm up. Stretch. 3 mile Yomp.
Day 4: Warm up. Stretch. Swim (375 metres, ie 15 lengths × 25 metres).
Day 5: Warm up. Stretch. Individual Circuit – 6 exercises in target time.
Day 6: Warm up. Stretch. 20 minute run. 20 minute cycle ride. 20 minute Yomp.
Day 7: Rest.

Notes:
Circuit: On Day 5, Week 4, re-test new circuit for a new target time. In the re-test, do the circuit 3 times through.
Run: You should be aiming for 10 minute miles (6 mph).
Yomp: The Marines aim consistently at a 20 minute mile (3 mph).

INDIVIDUAL CIRCUIT

Half Sit-ups
•
Dips
•
Step-ups
•
Dorsal Raises
•
Press-ups
•
Squats
(see pages 66–71)

Motivation Tips

- If you're a technical nut, make graphs of your weight, timings and measurements. This will encourage you to keep going.
- Try your hand at windsurfing. It is very hard work!
- When yomping in the autumn, take a basket as well as your pack and go mushroom picking in the woods. It makes time go faster and mushrooms are a great source of protein, carbohydrates, minerals and vitamins. Just make sure that you walk the right distance and don't pick poisonous mushrooms as eating them could set back your training some time (if in doubt consult a mushroom guide book).
- Make sure you are not just running on the flat. This gives a false sense of how well and how fast you are running as I know too well. The day before I began my Commando Tests, the officer in charge took us all for a 'quick run' – which consisted of 8 miles on Dartmoor roads and tracks. The first mile was straight up a long steep hill. Because my London training had all been on the flat, within 5 minutes I was 200 metres behind the rest of the batch, a gap I was never able – either physically or psychologically – to make up. By the end of the run, my confidence for the forthcoming tests was shattered.
- At the end of the Level, measure your waist, biceps and so on again. It should be proof that colleagues and friends who say you're looking fitter aren't saying it just to be nice.
- Go for a 'run ashore' to celebrate reaching Level 2. Or in civvy speak go out with some friends and have a few drinks. A change of scene does wonders for the outlook. However if the next morning is not a rest day, don't forego training. Running off a hangover is not very pleasant to begin with but more effective than Fernet Branca or a Bloody Mary.
- Keep smiling. Remember this is supposed to be fun . . . and you volunteered.

Test

Tests will be carried out on Day 6 of the third week. Before taking the Test, complete the Individual Circuit in target time.

The Test has four parts:

1 A 3 mile run to be completed in under 28 minutes.

2 A 30 minute cycle ride covering not less than 7 miles.

3 A 30 minute, 1½ mile Yomp.

4 15 Bastards (Burpees plus Star Jump – see illustration opposite). These should be done correctly – no short cuts and no cheating. For every incomplete one, do 2 more.

TEST EXERCISE
Bastards

The Bastard is a unique exercise to the Marines. For real authenticity, you should shout 'bastard' during the star jump.

- Stand erect.
- Go down into the squat position.
- Thrust both legs backwards to the press-ups position.
- Thrust both legs forwards to the squat position.

- Do a star jump, jumping as high as you can with arms and legs outstretched.
- Make sure you land on bent knees, and return to the squat position.
- Return to the starting position and stand erect.
- Repeat.

Nod

Congratulations! You have now become a Nod (marine slang for recruit). You are taking the programme seriously, and are perhaps even hooked on the idea of getting properly fit. Reward yourself by buying a new piece of kit. It doesn't have to be anything expensive – maybe a new pair of shorts or whatever you fancy. However, as distances and times increase you might consider investing £30 or so in a sports watch. In the middle of training my battered old watch gave up the ghost and I bought a superior replacement. It came complete with more functions than a NASA control panel including a lap counter, alarm and stopwatch. I find, especially when running, that I like to be able to track the time minute by minute, and once you start introducing exercise games to your routine, accurate timekeeping becomes essential.

Day 1: Warm up. Stretch. 40 minute run.
Day 2: Warm up. Stretch. Free choice circuit: choose 9 exercises (3 for arms, 3 for torso, 3 for legs – see pages 66–81). 15 repetitions of each. Rest for 1 minute. Then do another 15 repetitions of each exercise.
Day 3: Warm up. Stretch. 4 mile Yomp.
Day 4: Warm up. Stretch. Swim (500 metres, ie 20 lengths × 25 metres). 40 minute cycle ride (or 2 × 20 minute cycle rides to and from pool).
Day 5: Warm up. Stretch. Individual Circuit (9 exercises). 15 repetitions of each.
Day 6: Warm up. Stretch. 30 minute run. 30 minute cycle ride. 30 minute Yomp.
Day 7: Rest.

Notes:
Circuit: On Day 5, Week 7 re-test new circuit for a new target time.
Run: **1** At this stage you should be aiming for 8½ minute miles (7 mph).
     2 Change the patterns of your run by introducing new

A Nod's Bergen is his best friend, except when it is very heavy. To begin with, carrying over 50lbs in the pack is like the weight of the world on your shoulders. But by the end of training he will be capable of yomping for several days carrying over 100lbs.

INDIVIDUAL CIRCUIT

Half Sit-ups
•
Dips
•
Step-ups
•
Dorsal Raises
•
Press-ups
•
Squats
•
Sit-ups
•
Wide-arm Press-ups
•
Alternate Leg Squat Thrusts

(see pages 66–74)

games each week – first Fartlek (page 123), then Reverse Split (page 123) and to finish you off in Week 9 a session of Interval Running (pages 123–124).

3 Instead of your run on Day 6, do a Gridders session (page 121).

Yomp: **1** The Marines aim consistently at a 20 minute mile (3 mph). You should now increase the weight in your pack by a minimum 10 lbs.

2 Instead of the Yomp in Week 8, do a Hill Session (page 122).

3 Instead of the Yomp on Day 6, do a Leg Circuit following your Gridders session – then forget the cycle ride!

Swim: If it's getting boring introduce some games. Fartlek, Reverse Splits and Interval Running (pages 123–124) are just as valid – and exhausting – in the pool as on land.

MOTIVATION TIPS

● Start adding variations to your routine. Spice up simple runs with little games, swap a yomp for a leg circuit, a hill session or a visit down the local gym to do some weights. However don't forget the load carry altogether. Come the Commando Tests if you are not used to carrying that weight over inhospitable terrain, all the leg circuits in the world won't make it any easier. I know, from bitter experience.

● Don't lie about your personal achievements to yourself, and while to exaggerate to friends and colleagues is only human, an oft-repeated fib has a habit of becoming a universal belief. Don't claim to be a marathon runner until you've actually completed one; until that moment it is only an ambition.

● If you're feeling frustrated or annoyed after a row at the office or with your partner, channel that anger into something physical. Go for another run or cycle ride, or go play a game of squash. Don't feel that once you have completed the day's task, that's it. If you're up to more, then go for it.

● Remind yourself why you are doing the programme. Never forget your original aim. This always helps when you feel a bit down.

● Train with a partner as much as possible. This creates a healthy competitive attitude and one person can motivate the other on those off days.

● Keep setting yourself goals, both in the short term and the long

term. Make sure that they are achievable, not impossible pipe dreams. For example, your long-term goal might be to run a marathon in under 3½ hours, but in the short term you have to aim to be running consistent 9 minute miles; or you might want to trim a stone off that spare tyre. The Royal Marines Total Fitness Programme is designed to provide you with regular, attainable goals but add as many others as you want.

● Don't let training get in the way of your personal life. If you have a family or live-in partner involve them if you can. Let the kids cycle alongside while you run. Invite the wife to hold the stopwatch and crack the whip when you don't complete exercises properly.

● If you've never been skiing, try out a local dry ski slope. You will discover muscles in places you didn't know you had places.

● If you fancy burning off nervous energy, try rock climbing for a day.

● After completing this level take those measurements again on your waist, chest and biceps. Check how the graph is progressing. Pose in front of the mirror in your shorts and notice how your body is changing. I bet that makes you feel really good.

● Learn to be flexible. When I tore the muscles on my Achilles tendon and was condemned to 4 weeks in plaster just after I had reached peak fitness the most depressing factor to deal with was that I wanted to burn off my frustrations at being injured by running 8 miles and couldn't. It took nearly 2 weeks before I got rid of that anger and could channel it elsewhere. Eventually I just adapted my circuit to enable me to work daily on my abdomen and arms and did regular quad lifts with the plastered leg. It was 12 weeks before I could start running again and when I did it was only short distances. Initially I felt just like a saggy couch potato once again, but that soon passed.

Test

Tests will be carried out on Day 6 of the third week. Before taking the Test, complete the Individual Circuit in target time.

The Test has 4 parts:

1 A 4 mile run to be completed in under 34 minutes.

2 A 30 minute cycle ride covering not less than 8 miles.

3 A 40 minute Yomp covering not less than 2 miles.

4 20 full Bastards (Burpees plus press-up plus star jump – see overleaf). These should be done correctly – no short cuts and no cheating. For every incomplete one do 2 more. Don't forget to shout 'bastard' during the star jump!

TEST EXERCISE
Full Bastards

- Stand erect.
- Go down into the squat position.
- Thrust both legs backwards to the press-ups position.

- Lower your chest to the floor.
- Raise your chest up again.
- Thrust both legs forwards to the squat position.

- Do a star jump.
- Land with knees bent and go down into the squat position.
- Return to the starting position and stand erect.
- Repeat.

Marine

Congratulations! You have now become a Marine. Celebrate in time-honoured style by going out – get on down to the local club to boogie the night away. But remember there is more to life than the adrenalin high that hits after a good exercise session. Try to keep a balance between your life and your sport. Marines in training do not have this problem as there is always too much going on, too much kit to be cleaned and not enough time to get obsessed. Keep everything in balance and harmony. Consider taking an extra day off occasionally, when you can eat what you like or relax in front of a video. Try to spend more time than usual with your family and friends.

Day 1: Warm up. Stretch. 50 minute run.
Day 2: Warm up. Stretch. Free choice circuit: choose 9 exercises (3 for arms, 3 for torso, 3 for legs – see pages 66–81). 20 repetitions of each. Rest for 1 minute. Then do another 20 repetitions of each exercise.
Day 3: Warm up. Stretch. 5 mile Yomp.
Day 4: Warm up. Stretch. Swim (625 metres ie 25 lengths × 25 metres). 50 minute cycle ride.
Day 5: Warm up. Stretch. Individual Circuit: 13 exercises. 3 repetitions of each.
Day 6: Warm up. Stretch. 40 minute run. 40 minute cycle ride. 40 minute Yomp.
Day 7: Rest, except in Week 12 when you take the Test.

Notes:
Circuit: On Day 5, Week 10 re-test new circuit for a new target time.
Run: At this stage you should aim for 8 minute miles (7½ mph).
Yomp: The Marines aim consistently at a 20 minute mile (3 mph), but you should now increase the weight in your pack by a further 10 lbs.
Swim: 1 Breaststroke exercises the whole body better than crawl – which is better for speed and stamina. For the best mix, alternate strokes every five lengths.

Once IMF is completed, a Nod heads for the Bottom Field to begin Battle Field Training. Now he carries his weapon and 'fighting order' (22lbs in pouches) and carries out all the exercises in his boots. A fireman's carry may not seem too hard – unless you have to run 60 yards in under 30 seconds.
Picture by Matthew Ford

INDIVIDUAL CIRCUIT

Half Sit-ups
●
Dips
●
Step-ups
●
Dorsal Raises
●
Press-ups
●
Squats
●
Sit-ups
●
Wide-arm Press-ups
●
Alternate Leg Squat Thrusts
●
Sit-ups with a Twist
●
Dorsals
●
Squat Thrusts
●
V-Sits

(see pages 66–78)

2 Every other week try an individual medley: 4 lengths of each stroke – including backstroke and butterfly – finished off with five lengths flat out crawl.

Variations: In Level 3 you may have tried various running and swimming games to spice up the training, to add variation and save time now that the yomps are getting longer. If you haven't done so before now, introduce them into your weekly routine, but don't overdo it. Remember that there is no effective substitute to yomping with a pack – everything else is too comfortable.

MOTIVATION TIPS

● Go for a gentle walk, stop and take in the scenery. Next time you go for a yomp, take a similar route and admire it once again.

● Once the distances for running, cycling and yomping get longer, you will soon become accustomed to relaxing. Part of your mind will always be alert for stray cats, potholes or homicidal buses but let your legs take the strain. There are all sorts of memory games to play, lists to compile. One of my favourites is choosing my selection of eight records for the BBC 4 radio programme Desert Island Discs, though the luxury item still eludes me. Or you might like to try to select a United Kingdom soccer team. The secret is to relax and because you are running a familiar route you can let your mind wander a little. Even work problems can be chewed over in an alien environment. Away from office pressure, satisfactory solutions can often be reached.

● It's a day to go running and the weather's doing a Dartmoor Special – it's clagged in, pouring with rain and freezing. It would be easy to stay indoors, maybe do an extra circuit instead. But test your commitment by doing that run. After the first few minutes you won't feel the damp and you will feel a tremendous sense of achievement when you get home.

● Always stay hydrated. Get into the habit of drinking water – at least 5 litres a day. Remember coffee and tea are diuretics that make you urinate more frequently. The easiest way to check is to look at the colour of your urine. The yellower it is the more dehydrated you are. It can take over two hours to fully hydrate the body.

● Play a competitive game instead of one of the daily disciplines – squash, badminton, basketball, soccer or whatever you enjoy (see page 142). It will maintain your fitness but relieves the pressure of the programme and helps combat boredom. The aim is to raise the heartbeat.

● Take your bike over some rough ground for 30 minutes of cyclocross. Then spend a relaxing hour maintaining your bike, cleaning off the

mud and generally taking care of it. Always keep all your kit clean and in working order.

● Monitor your pulse rates over a week. Now look back at your notes and compare the difference with J Week.

● The longer the run, the more the chances are that you are pushing your body to the limits. 'Hitting the wall' can be largely eliminated by good nutrition and eating properly (see pages 115–119).

Coping with blisters

Treat blisters early. Everyone has favoured methods. During my Commando Test Week I picked up some serious blisters on the load carry and was given an old fashioned Marine treatment which I do not recommend except in dire emergency. The blister liquid is drawn out with a plastic hypodermic and replaced with Tinc Benzine, a thick brown caustic agent with the ability to make a man's head hit the ceiling from a seated position. It really hurts but is effective in that you can continue your yomp or run within minutes.

Another effective method is to take a sterilized needle and thread, pierce both sides of the blister and leave half a centimetre of thread hanging out of each end. This drains the blister slowly and lets the flesh inside dry.

Better still is prevention. Keep your feet dry and warm. Use foot powder regularly to prevent rubbing, then cover the more sensitive, vulnerable areas of each foot with zinc oxide tape.

Test

The Test for Level 4 is different and is to take place on Day 7 of Week 12, assuming you have reached the target time on your Individual Circuit. Day 6 remains as usual. Sorry about that Rest Day!

The Test has only 2 parts:

1 Retake the Initial Fitness Test (page 21). You must score a total of over 200 points.

2 Run the 1½ miles in under 10 minutes.

Commando

Congratulations! You have become a Commando. You are certainly now fit enough to exert more control over your exercise programme, so by all means introduce variations if you wish. But keep the core recommended here if you are aiming to crack the Tests. These do not simply determine whether you are physically fit but that you are also hewn from the right stuff. The Commando Level exercise programme is very hard work but if you've got this far it's going to take a runaway truck to stop you finishing now. Keep everything else in perspective. Take a deep breath, and go for it!

When a Marine begins his month long Commando Course he is introduced to the delights of the Endurance Course – 2 miles of mud, tunnels and the Water Tunnel where he has to completely submerge himself and be pulled through a 6 foot concrete tube by his partners. Soaked through, he only has another 5 miles to go and only 72 minutes to complete the whole thing.

Day 1: Warm up. Stretch. 60 minute/8 mile run.
Day 2: Warm up. Stretch. Free choice circuit: choose 12 exercises (4 for arms, 4 for torso, 4 for legs – see pages 66–81). 20 repetitions of each. Rest for 2 minutes. Then do another 20 repetitions of each exercise.
Day 3: Warm up. Stretch. 8 mile Yomp.
Day 4: Warm up. Stretch. Swim (750 metres ie 30 lengths × 25 metres). 60 minute cycle ride.
Day 5: Warm up. Stretch. Individual Circuit (all 16 exercises). 3 repetitions of each.
Day 6: Warm up. Stretch. 45 minute run. 45 minute cycle ride. 60 minute Yomp. 750 metre swim (30 lengths × 25 metres).
Day 7: Rest.

INDIVIDUAL CIRCUIT
●
(see overleaf for exercises)

Notes:
Circuit: On Day 5, Week 13 re-test new circuit for a new target time.
Run: At this stage you should aim for 7½ minute miles (8 mph).
Yomp: The Marines aim consistently at a 20 minute mile (3 mph). You should now increase the weight in your pack by a further 10 lbs.
Swim: 1 Breaststroke exercises the whole body better than crawl – which is better for speed and stamina. For the best mix, alternate strokes every five lengths.
     2 On alternate weeks try an individual medley, 6 lengths of

each stroke – including backstroke and butterfly – finished off with 6 lengths flat out crawl.

Variations: You are now fit enough to have more control over your personal programme. However for every three week period you spend in Level 5 you should make sure you do at least 2 Yomps, 1 Interval Training, 1 Hill Session, 1 Gridders, 2 Leg Circuits (see pages 121–124).

MOTIVATION TIPS

● Don't become obsessed with training – it must remain enjoyable.
● Visit your local gym or fitness centre and work out on all the machines – but ask advice from the assistants before loading half a ton of weights on to the leg raise. If you aren't used to lifting weights, do loads of repetitions on lower settings.
● Try an aerobics or step aerobics exercise session. You will be amazed at how difficult it can be. It might also make you respect your wife or girlfriend more.
● If you are near a beach, run up and down the dunes for 15 minutes. Then go for a swim – not a paddle – in the sea.

Using isotonic drinks on long distance runs

Many fluid replacement drinks are now available. They range from old favourites like Lucozade Isotonic to such American imports as Ultra Fuel or Hyper Fuel which fortunately taste better than their luminous green colour might suggest. You can also buy powders like Isostar which you mix yourself. Whether they actually work is a matter of opinion but if you do mix up your own make sure you follow the instructions exactly; if you get the balance wrong the drink might dehydrate you and that could be dangerous.

In my experience the use of isotonic drinks is primarily psychological. When I did a 30 Miler on a scorching June day, I was loaded down with fluids. From 9.00 am the previous morning – when we had completed the 9 mile speed march – until we went to bed, we were sipping liquids, ranging from flat Coca-Cola to water, from Murphy's Stout to Isostar that seemed to taste of old bath water. The immediate result was that I spent most of a sleepless night padding to and from the lavatory but I was extremely hydrated when we began at 5.30 in the morning. Most of my weight was taken up with fluids – one water bottle, one water bottle full of Hyper Fuel and three pouches of Lucozade Isotonic. Thirty miles later I had drunk gallons of water, two Lucozades

INDIVIDUAL CIRCUIT

Half Sit-ups
•
Dips
•
Step-ups
•
Dorsal Raises
•
Press-ups
•
Squats
•
Sit-ups
•
Wide-arm Press-ups
•
Alternate Leg Squat Thrusts
•
Sit-ups with a Twist
•
Dorsals
•
Squat Thrusts
•
V-Sits
•
Clap Press-ups
•
Tuck Jumps
•
Crunchies

(see pages 66–81)

and most of the Hyper Fuel. I used the drinks as a goal – so after 3 hours I allowed myself a Lucozade. Any effect they had was probably only short term, if better than eating a Mars Bar which after an initial sugar hit is followed by a depression.

These days I stick with a Mars Bar for resting only and have a can of chilled Lucozade Lemon and Lime Isotonic after completing exercise . . . and that is because I like the taste!

Test

The Test will be carried out on Day 6. Before taking the Test, complete the Individual Circuit in target time.

The Test has 5 parts:

1 An 8 mile run to be completed in under 59 minutes.
2 A 60 minute cycle ride covering not less than 18 miles.
3 A Yomp of not less than 4 miles.
4 A 75 metre swim (30 lengths × 25 metres).
5 20 Full Bastards with a clap (Burpees plus press-up with a clap plus star jump – see pages 104–105).

These should be done correctly – no short cuts and no cheating. For every incomplete one do 2 more. If you still have the energy and breath to shout 'bastard' during the star jump, you are really fit.

TEST EXERCISE
Full Bastards with a Clap

- Stand erect.
- Go down into the squat position.
- Thrust both legs backwards to the press-ups position.

- Lower your chest towards, but do not touch, the floor.
- Push up off the floor and clap your hands.
- Make sure you land on bent arms.
- Raise chest up to press-ups position, with straight arms.
- Thrust both legs forwards to the squat position.

- Do a star jump. Land on bent knees and go down to the squat position.
- Return to the starting position and stand erect.
- Repeat.

Test Week

The Test at the end of Level 5 is probably harder than those in the upcoming Test Week. All athletes overtrain but now you are ready. That should make you feel better.

Training culminates in a 'Commando Test Week', based as closely as possible on the actual Tests used by the Marines to determine whether a recruit is worthy of being awarded his green beret. Some of the tests cannot be transferred into civilian terms so alternatives have been substituted.

Ideally the Commando Tests should be conducted over four consecutive days. Where this is not practical, the tests can be conducted over two consecutive weekends.

Knee-deep in mud, soaked to the skin and there are only another 20 miles to go. The 30 Miler is the ultimate Commando Test over unforgiving Dartmoor Terrain in unpredictable weather. They have to run downhill and on the flat (but there isn't any) and walk up the hills carrying 'fighting order' and their weapon in under 8 hours. The reward at the end is enough . . . the green beret.

Test 1 Twelve mile load carry

A 12 mile Yomp to be completed in under 4 hours. The test is to be conducted in boots, on roads, or paths, carrying a rucksack weighing not less than 70 lbs. (The Marines carry 70 lbs plus their rifle which weighs a further 10 lbs.) If a woman takes this test she should only carry a total of 40–50 lbs maximum.

Test 2 Swimming test

Swim 500 metres in less than 10 minutes (400 metres in under 8 minutes is a basic Special Boat Service Test). You can choose any stroke you like, but remember crawl is faster than breaststroke.

Test 3 Endurance test

This is a three part test:
1   Step-ups – 100 on each leg.
    Sit-ups – 100.
    Press-ups – 50.
2   A 5 mile cycle ride.
3   A 6 mile run.

All three parts of the Endurance Test must be completed in under 72 minutes.

Note: the Swimming Test and the Endurance Test must be completed in the same day.

Test 4 Nine mile speed march

You must cover 9 miles in 90 minutes, wearing boots and carrying a pack weighing 22 lbs. The entire march can take place on roads and/or tarmac paths but the terrain should vary from the flat to quite steep climbs and descents. Keep the pace to a fast jog.

Test 5 Thirty miler

This is the ultimate Commando Test: 30 miles across rough terrain, wearing boots and carrying a 30 lb pack. Complete this in under 8 hours.

Tips for tests

- The day before the 30 Miler, aim to spend the entire day relaxing and stocking up with fuel, so start the 9 miler early to allow maximum recovery time. In other words eat as much as you can both at lunch and supper, concentrating on storing up carbohydrates like a squirrel stores its nuts for winter (see pages 115–119 for advice on the right foodstuffs). Also drink constantly to make sure you do not get dehydrated on the day.
- Avoid blisters. If your boots are properly worn in, blisters should not be a problem. However before going on any speed march or long hike, action towards prevention is time well spent. Buy some zinc oxide tape and cover your ankles, heels, big toes and any other areas that rub. I covered every toe except one and after the 30 Miler that was so blistered that I lost the toe-nail. If you get blisters on the first couple of days and cannot face the Tinc Benzine ordeal, some chemists do stock 'Second Skin' – clear plastic film that sets hard and protects the feet so you can continue. At this stage dropping out because of blisters is unacceptable, so don't leave anything to chance.
- Before embarking on the 30 Miler, make sure that you know your route well, that you have a map and compass and that your pack contains waterproofs, a change of clothes, socks, and – depending on the time of year – hats and gloves. Take plenty of water and high energy foods –

power bars, Mars Bars, raisins – that don't weigh a ton.

Rules for the 30 Miler:

1 Recce the route properly in advance. Build in certain checkpoints that are easily accessible by road.

2 Do not go alone across rough country.

3 Start as early in the morning as you can, depending on the season. Beginning just before dawn is preferable to trying to finish in the dark as you are more likely to make mistakes when you are tired.

4 Inform friends of approximately when you expect to be passing checkpoints. Ask them to be waiting with supplies of water, plasters and so on.

5 If the weather clags in, or you get hopelessly lost, head for the nearest human habitation or tarmac road, and wait there. Don't try to be a Captain Oates. You can always try again in more favourable weather.

Staying Fit

OK, so you've achieved total fitness now . . . or think you have. But how do you stay that way for life? It should be easy enough because you have already done all the hard work. All you need to do is find two and a half hours every week to maintain your fitness level.

Let's suppose you've reached Level 4, but for a variety of reasons – time, work or family pressure, or maybe you feel you've proved yourself already – you don't want to go the whole hog and train up to take the Commando Tests. However, you do feel better than you ever have before, you've lost 10 lbs and there is a spring to your step and a glint in your eye that wasn't there three months ago. Obviously you want to keep that, but you don't want to become a born-again fitness addict.

It may sound strange, coming at this stage after a pretty gruelling training programme but there is more to life than physical exercise. The Marines' training is designed for a specific purpose – they are the Navy's soldiers and only when their training is complete are they ready to carry out their appointed tasks, to do their jobs. You're still a civvy – albeit a fit civvy – and should never lose that perspective.

Many people are just as addicted to exercise as heroin addicts are to heroin or alcoholics to alcohol. When I was in the full flood of my training I would sometimes hear myself at parties expounding on the joys of hard exercise with all the fervour of a religious convert. Avoid becoming a born-again exercise bore at all costs. It is a fine line that not all Marines escape. Stories abound of officers addicted to running 20 miles a day, every day of the year including Christmas, or sergeants who spend every spare minute pressing enormous weights in the gym. Always keep having a healthy body in perspective.

Once you have achieved that goal you originally set yourself, your hard-earned fitness can vanish a lot quicker than it came. Professional athletes can take up to three weeks off training and within a couple of days will be close to where they were before they took a break. But if a 'fat civvy' slobs out for much more than a week, it might take some hard graft to get back on track. However don't be put off from taking a two-week holiday because the chances are that you will do some exercise – a little light windsurfing, the odd jog, tennis or golf – because by now it is

Once a Marine has earned his green beret, the real soldiering begins. Carrying huge logs and heavy pipes through tropical rainforest requires just as much physical commitment . . . but this time it's for real and there may be someone shooting at him.

so ingrained in your physical makeup that you fret a bit if you're not sweating. Most important of all you need to relax occasionally. A good time unwinding can be worth a week's hard exercise.

Scientific research has shown that the absolute minimum exercise to maintain your level of physical fitness should be 20 minutes three times a week, where the heart rate has risen to 60–85 per cent of its maximum heart rate. For a variety of reasons Marine PTIs do not consider this to be sufficient. Instead they recommend a weekly cycle of five days exercising, two days resting (but not consecutively) and that the heart should be beating at 60–85 per cent of its MHR for a minimum of 30 minutes. Don't forget that even when you are exercising less, you should never omit the warm-ups, stretches and warm-downs.

Planning your own programme

If you have reached Level 3, and want to take things easier for a few weeks but not lose the rhythm of the Royal Marines Total Fitness Programme, the simplest way do do it is to continue to follow the exercises in Level 3 but do them every other day, or even at a pinch every third day. That way you will maintain your fitness level without losing your pace and place in the programme. However, if and when you want to resume the programme proper, you must go back to the daily routine and pass the Level 3 Test before progressing further.

Having completed Level 3 you will now know what form of exercise you like doing best, what your body likes best and what you are capable of. The three are not necessarily the same! It's up to you to work out your own programme, and be sensible and committed enough to carry it out.

Choose which forms of aerobic and strength exercises you have enjoyed most so far – whether it be swimming, circuit training, running, cycling, yomping or lifting weights – and design your own programme around that. For extra variations see pages 142–143 for advice on how different sports can fit into your plans. Always warm up and stretch first. Then make sure you get the heart beating and the sweat coming for a minimum of 30 minutes. Then warm down gradually. Keep to this for five hours a week and you will never regret it. Don't forget to check your pulse rate regularly.

Base your programme around the following seven-day cycle:

Day 1: Aerobic – running, swimming, or cycling.
Day 2: Strength – circuit training, weight training or load carrying.
Day 3: Aerobic.
Day 4: Rest.
Day 5: Aerobic.
Day 6: Strength.
Day 7: Rest.

Example

After I finished my Commando Tests I immediately discarded yomping from my strength schedule as I found it to be both boring and time consuming. I replaced it with a mixture of general circuit work, leg circuits, the occasional hill session (but only occasional as they are very tiring) and some weightlifting with a home dumbbell set for the upper body. For aerobic work I cycled to work and ran for pleasure (something of a turn around since as recently as two years ago I would announce to all and sundry that running was the dullest sport in the world . . . except for golf).

Swimming was also dropped because I found it uninspiring . . . until I tore the muscles in my calf and had to reconstruct an exercise programme around swimming. For six weeks after the accident I was able to do very little exercise except for dozens of tummy exercises and a bit of upper body weight training and press-ups, which was incredibly frustrating. Being able to go into the water was a tremendous relief because it allowed me both the luxury and psychological confidence of being able to move my left leg normally. The water supported the leg, although initially even a 20 minute session of swimming and exercises in neck-deep water was more tiring than a 10 mile run had been before. It was a further six weeks before I could very gingerly go on a run. By that time, of course, I was enjoying swimming, even using some of the games like Fartlek and reverse splits to liven up the alternate lengths of breaststroke and crawl. It all goes to show that you can adapt your training programme to fit changed circumstances. But only so long as you want to.

Diet:
food for training

Over the last decade it has been acknowledged by everyone from government agencies to the food industry that good nutrition – sensible eating, if you like – has a positive impact on health and fitness. There is clear evidence to show that improved eating habits not only benefit health but also influence a person's capacity to perform exercise.

While strength, endurance, flexibility, speed and power are all improved by structured specific training like the Royal Marines Total Fitness Programme, such physical abilities can all be fortified by sensible eating.

Your diet consists of six basic categories:

1 Carbohydrates

For distance running the body needs carbohydrates. There are two main high carbohydrate foods: starch foods like pasta, wholemeal bread, cereals and pulses (which also contain other vitamins and minerals) and sugary foods in which the carbohydrates have been extracted and broken down so that they can be quickly absorbed into the digestive system. The disadvantage with sweets, sugary drinks, and biscuits is that they can also contain a lot of fat and very few other essential nutrients. If you are serious about training, try to cut your sugar content in half.

Ideally you should aim to replace foods rich in fat and sugar with low-fat foods. Your body will continue to absorb energy from unprocessed food sources like potatoes, fruit and vegetables. This will also increase your intake of fibre which is good for the digestion. Carbohydrate is transformed into glycogen for use as fuel, but if not used is stored in the liver as a form of fat.

Eating out in the wild isn't all bad, provided a Marine has his 24-hour ration packs, his waterproof matches, and his hexamine blocks to heat up a mess tin so he can always brew up a 'hot wet'. However, sometimes he has to survive on his own initiative when anything and everything can find themselves on the menu.
Picture by Matthew Ford

2 Fat

There continues to be much debate about whether fat is bad for you. Similarly, whether or not it is better to eat unsaturated (vegetable oils and fats) or saturated (meat) fats remains opens to discussion. The link between a high cholesterol count and heart disease has been established but then the healthiest people in France live in the Dordogne on a diet which appears to be based on goose fat and red wine! Seriously though, those very people are also farmers, highly active for most of the year with an innate ability to relax stress away.

Fats are important sources of energy but the British probably consume too much for their own good. In other words, approach the great British cooked breakfast with caution, especially if you aren't taking enough exercise to burn it off. You don't really start to burn fat until you have been exercising for over 90 minutes.

3 Proteins

To get technical, proteins are broken down in the gut into amino acids. There are twenty-one amino acids of which the body cannot make at least eight. These are known as essential amino acids and you must include them in your diet. Amino acids are needed to manufacture the components of tissues such as muscles, and under extreme conditions they may be used to provide energy. However, there is little evidence to suggest you need to increase your normal protein intake even during very heavy training.

4 Vitamins

Signs of scurvy or other vitamin deficiencies are seldom seen in western countries today. Recent surveys show that 30–80 per cent of all athletes regularly take vitamin and mineral supplements, working on the assumption that if some vitamins are involved in energy metabolism, increasing the dosage will improve performance. However, scientific findings suggest that vitamin supplementation has no meaningful effect on performance. You only need to eat a sensible variety of foods to get the necessary vitamins into your system.

5 Minerals

The human body is 5 per cent minerals, and these are essential to the maintenance of nerve and muscle function. Iron is a major nutrient because of the vital role it plays in metabolism and the body's capacity to perform muscular work. Eat lots of beans, green leafy vegetables, whole grains with the odd serving of liver (which tastes much better if you don't overcook it) and that should satisfy your body's requirements.

6 Water

It may seem pretty obvious but water provides the body's main transportation system conveying nutrients, waste products and hormones to the right places. It also helps to control the body's temperature – sweating during exercise results in the body cooling. But do be aware that even small losses of water (2–3 per cent loss of body weight) can seriously hinder performance. Stay hydrated!

Top Ten Foods for Runners

Any athlete preparing for a big race – especially a distance run – will spend the day before loading up on carbohydrates and other essential nutrients. However, it is counterproductive to eat junk food for weeks before the moment of truth and then decide to become a health food nut! It is far better to eat sensibly throughout training. The following is a rough guide to the best type of foodstuffs available to help maximize your potential. More specific recommendations for how to prepare for the 30 Miler will be found in the Commando Test Week chapter (page 101).

1 Pasta (spaghetti, macaroni, lasagne, tagliatelle etc.)
FOR: Pasta is the ideal fuel for runners because it is high in complex carbohydrates. Low in fat with a high fibre content, it is a slow release food that provides many basic nutrients. It is also filling, easy to prepare and inexpensive.
AGAINST: Choose the sauce carefully – covering the pasta with fatty cheese or mince is counterproductive. You need carbohydrates for energy and not fat.

2 Oats (muesli etc.)
FOR: A bowl of warm porridge or muesli is a much better breakfast than a fry-up. Packed with carbohydrates and full of B vitamins, oats are low in fat and provide essential roughage.
AGAINST: Not a lot.

3 Wholemeal Bread
FOR: Often called the staff of life, bread contains all the basic elements for a healthy diet in the right ratios. Every meal should contain a slice or two.
AGAINST: White bread and coloured brown bread contain additives, preservatives and salt as well as being lower in vitamins. Try to avoid covering that wholemeal slice with lashings of butter and jam!

HEALTHY EATING TIPS

Control your energy intake.

●

Eat less fat, particularly saturated fats.

●

Eat more starchy foods rich in fibre.

●

Eat less refined and processed sugar.

●

Eat less salt.

●

Drink less alcohol.

A well-balanced diet contains 75 per cent carbohydrates (complex), 15 per cent protein and 10 per cent fat.

---

4 Beans and Pulses

FOR: The vegetarian's perfect alternative to meat, these are high in protein, very filling . . . and cheap. Bags of beans can be kept in the larder for ages. They are easy to prepare and can be very tasty. There are over twenty types, opening endless cooking opportunities.

AGAINST: A bit inflexible. Because they usually have to be soaked overnight, meals have to be planned in advance.

5 Yogurt

FOR: Among the most refreshing foods around, capable of taking the burn off a Vindaloo curry! But be careful to choose low-fat, additive-free natural yogurts which contain calcium, three vitamins and potassium.

AGAINST: Can be expensive and commercial yogurts are full of sugar, preservatives and fat.

6 Dried Fruit

FOR: A healthier alternative to plain sugar when added to cereals and bread. The ideal handy after-run treat and a useful snack. Dried apricots, bananas, raisins, figs and peaches are just part of the vast range available.

AGAINST: Be warned you can over-consume because they taste so good!

7 Potatoes

FOR: As much sinned against as sinner, the humble spud has its critics but is in fact high in vitamin C and very low in fat.

AGAINST: How you cook them. Frying or roasting increases the fat content so stick to boiled and baked which retain higher amounts of vitamins and minerals, and refrain from serving them with butter.

8 Fish

FOR: The Wonder Food? Fish is full of essential oils, high in protein and vitamins, easy to cook and tasty to eat. It is always better to grill or poach fish than fry it in batter. If you have to fry, use the fish's natural oils. Recent medical research has shown that oily fish like mackerel and salmon are particularly good for reducing cholesterol levels.

AGAINST: Can be smelly and fiddly to prepare, but most towns now have a good fishmonger where fresh fish are readily available. Check the eyes – if the stare is really glassy the fish has been out of the water for too long. Pre-packed or frozen fish make an acceptable alternative.

9 Bananas

FOR: Nature's snack gift to runners, complete with environmentally friendly biodegradable packaging. High in carbohydrates, easy to eat on the move and cheap. The perfect, quick, tasty, healthy runners' anti-wall food. High in potassium, with useful amounts of vitamin C.

AGAINST: Watch out for slippery skins!

10 Mushrooms

FOR: Now available all year round in different varieties, these edible fungi are often neglected. Easy to prepare or eat raw in salads, they contain useful minerals and vitamins and can be the basis of excellent sauces to accompany pasta.

AGAINST: If you start running in autumn woodlands, the run can degenerate into a fungi picking foray! Watch out for the poisonous or hallucinogenic kind as they can play havoc with your training schedule.

TOP TEN CHART

(Based on 100 grams of foodstuff, all figures in grams except for calories. T = Trace)

FOOD	PROTEIN	FAT	FIBRE	CARBOHYDRATES	CALORIES
Pasta	15.2	3	none	65	347
Oats	12.4	8.7	7	72	400
Bread	8.8	2.7	8.5	41.8	216
Beans (pulses)	22	1.7	25	45	270
Yogurt (low fat)	5	low	none	6.2	52
Dried fruit	8	0	none	64.4	240
Potatoes	1.2	T	2	18	120
Fish (Tuna)	28	6	none	none	185
Bananas	1	T	2	10	110
Mushrooms	4	T	2	30	4

Alternative Exercises

You can substitute various exercises to the normal routine you have used. They are most useful as alternatives to the long distance yomps that start in Level 3 and for spicing up the runs with games that can be played as you jog. There is also a very approximate guide to playing other sports without interrupting your training programme.

GRIDDERS AND HILL SESSIONS

Gridders (Marine speak for 'grid sprints') and hill sessions are useful alternatives to a long run or yomp if time is short. However they are anaerobic exercises (which means the body is being pushed to its very limits, starving the heart and brain of oxygen) and therefore each one should not be carried out more than once in every three week Level.

While they could be carried out in Levels 1 and 2 they are only introduced into the programme at Level 3.

GRIDDERS

Find a flat space of ground, indoors or outdoors, that measures 20 metres. Mark every 5 metres (anything will do – a jumper, a road beacon, this book – it is only a mark, not a hurdle).
You can either do gridders Short then Long, or Long then Short.

Short then Long:
1 Run from start line to 5 metre mark and back.
 Run from start line to 10 metre mark and back.
 Run from start line to 15 metre mark and back.
 Run from start line to 20 metre mark and back.
2 Rest for 30 seconds then repeat.
3 Rest for 30 seconds.
 Sprint from start line to 10 metre mark and back.
 Sprint from start line to 20 metre mark and back.

Falling down cliff faces is one way to keep fit, but Marines have to learn to trust each other. This young officer has jumped out from a Dartmoor cliff relying on the brakeman at the bottom to halt his descent. It must have been something he said earlier! Don't try this at home.
Picture by Robin Eggar

4 Long Ones:

Sprint from start line to 20 metre mark and back three times.

5 Take up to 2 minutes breather then repeat up to 3 times depending on fitness level.

Long then Short: Not surprisingly, start with the 3 × 20 metre mark sprints (step 4) and do the cycle in reverse.

Warning: Doing this too much is counterproductive as it is anaerobic and can lead to oxygen starvation in the blood.

HILL SESSION

This makes an excellent occasional alternative to the Yomp/Load Carry as it exercises both the legs and the heart. First find a hill with a clear running area up to 100 metres long. The gradient should be 1 in 5 or 1 in 6 inches – not too steep.

Level 1

1 Start running at the bottom at a steady pace that increases to become progressively faster and harder by the time you reach the top.

2 Slow jog down followed by 30 seconds breather.

3 Repeat twice.

Levels 2–4

1 Run up and jog down the hill (as above) three times without stopping. Rest for 2 minutes.

2 Repeat twice.

Level 5

1 Do the exercise nine times without a breather.

On all Levels, after completing the hill session take a two minute breather, then do a few circuit exercises (pages 66–81), to build up back strength (halve the amounts if you are at Level 1). End the circuit with

10 Advanced Dorsals (page 133).

10 Press-ups (page 70).

10 Half Sit-ups (page 66).

LEG CIRCUIT

1 Choose six leg only exercises (see pages 66–81). More exercises can be found on pages 125–141.

2 Do 10–12 repetitions of each, but do a blast, work hard and work fast.

3 Take a 2 minute breather, but keep moving all the time, then repeat circuit.

4 Take a 2 minute breather, but keep moving, then repeat circuit.

The next time you do the leg circuit, choose a different set of exercises.

WATER RUNNING

This is a Load Carry and Swimming alternative. It is also good for anyone recovering from injury – especially if you are suffering from knee pains and shin splints – as the water supports damaged tissue all over but the movement does not stop the blood flowing to the muscles.

1 Stand in the shallow end of the pool and do your stretching exercises (see pages 48–57), avoiding those which would take you under water.

2 Spend 15 minutes running across the shallow end and back, using normal arm and leg movements as far as possible.

3 If the pool provides a garment called a Wet Vest – it helps you float – run the entire length of the pool wearing it. This is particularly good if you are recovering from a chronic injury.

RUNNING ALTERNATIVES

After a while you may get bored with running the same old route, week in week out. One solution is to change your route but here are three alternatives designed to reduce boredom while increasing stamina and fitness. You can also play any of these games in the swimming pool.

1 Fartlek (Swedish for Speed Play)

Basically you run as you please, but by throwing in different spontaneous choices you keep yourself on the tip of those jogging shoes.

For example you vary the pace, or decide to sprint the first 400 metres of your route, or take the hill incline at full speed. Play tag with every other lamp post, or even play jump the lines on paving stones like you did as a kid. It may seem strange to passers by but it may cheer you up as you build on your speed and strength.

2 Reverse Split

Pick a regular route that you know roughly how long it takes you to run and work out the exact half-way point. Time your route out, and then make sure you come back faster, not just by seconds but by minutes.

Example: The route takes you on average 39–41 minutes. The outward leg you run in 19 minutes. Your target for the return is under 17 minutes.

3 Interval Running on a Track

This is extremely hard training and should not be carried out more than once a week. (Do it once and you'll know why.)

Visit your local track and divide the distance you are supposed to run into different intervals (400, 800 or 1000 metres, for example).

Let us suppose you have a 3 mile run split into 10 × 400 metre intervals.

1 Run the first 400 metres at full speed.

2 Recovery time (see below). Then run the next 400 metres at full speed.

3 Repeat until the whole distance has been covered (or you collapse, whichever is sooner).

There are two ways of working on the recovery time. The easy option is to keep it variable; only go again when you have your breath back and your heart rate is approaching its normal working rate. The harder way is to have a fixed recovery time. But be careful – the longer the distances you run, the longer the breather should be (eg 400 metres = 30 seconds, 1000 metres = 2 minutes).

Additional Circuit Exercises

Here are some extra circuit exercises to increase your options and to help combat boredom. Some do require extra equipment like weights, a pull-up bar and a sturdy bench but if you don't want to buy them look around for alternatives (most parks will have a children's playground where the swings or climbing frames make excellent pull-up bars).

In general these exercises are harder than the originals. Some make me wince just describing them, so approach at your leisure and with caution. Remember that no matter how fit you are, learning a new exercise takes time.

For the first three arm exercises use individual dumb-bells, a barbell or even make your own weights with a broom handle and two paint cans weighted with gravel. Don't add too much weight – keep it between 10–20 kilos maximum. When picking up or putting down weights, always bend the knees not the torso, keep the back straight, and head up. Hold weights by gripping them tightly and always keep the wrists locked – don't flex them. As you do these arm exercises, there should be no excessive movement of the elbows.

Bicep Curls (A)

- Sit on the edge of a chair with feet wide apart and rest your left elbow on your knee. Grip the dumb-bell tightly with your right hand. Your right arm is bent and the elbow is pushing against the inside of your right knee.
- Keeping your right elbow as still as possible, fully extend your right forearm down towards the floor. Do not lock the elbow. Bring your forearm back up to the starting position and repeat.
- Repeat with the left arm and do an equal number of repetitions to each side.

Tricep Presses (A)

- Sit on a chair with your back straight and feet hip-width apart. Holding the dumb-bell in your right hand, bring your right elbow close to your head and place the dumb-bell between your shoulder blades. Place your left hand on your chest.
- Keeping the elbow as still as possible, extend your right forearm up towards the ceiling, raising the dumb-bell as high as you can. Do not lock your elbow. Bring your forearm back down, so that it rests once again between your shoulder blades and repeat.
- Repeat with the left arm and do an equal number of repetitions to each side.

Double Lateral Raises (A)

- Stand with feet shoulder-width apart, knees slightly bent, and hold a dumb-bell in each hand.
- Extend both arms out to the sides bringing the dumb-bells up to shoulder level.
- Bring your arms back down to the starting position and repeat.

Raised Leg Press-Ups (A)

● Place the balls of your feet on a 12-inch high platform or bench and do the press-ups from this position.

For a more advanced version, try the Alternate Raised Leg Press-Up.
● Start in the standard press-ups position (arms below shoulders).
● As you bend your arms to lower your chest, raise your right leg off the floor. As you raise the chest, lower the leg once again to the floor.

● Repeat, raising the left leg and do further repetitions raising alternate legs.

Underarm Pull-Ups (A)

- Stand facing a pull-up bar and grip it tightly with both hands. Your arms should be straight with the palms of your hands facing you.
- Using the strength of your arms pull yourself up off the floor until your chin is above the bar.
- Lower yourself back to the floor and repeat.

Reverse Sit-Ups (T)

For this exercise you may need a partner to hold your feet down. Alternatively, hook your feet under a sofa or bed.

● Sit up straight on a platform or bench with your feet together and flat on the floor, held down by your partner. Place your hands on your temples.

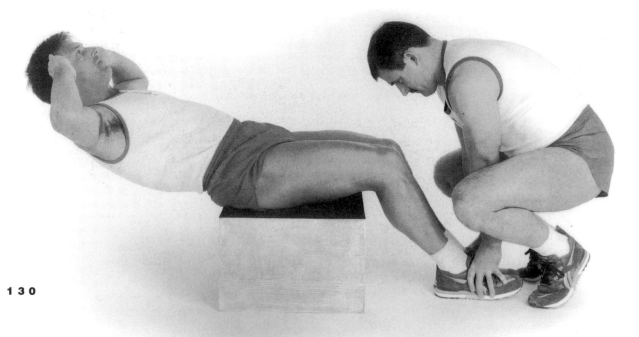

● Lie back to a horizontal position.
● Return to the starting position and repeat.

Flutter Kicks (T)

- Lie on the floor with knees bent, heels on the floor and toes raised. Place your hand underneath the small of your back and support your weight on your forearms.
- Raise both legs and kick alternate legs upwards as if you were doing the crawl. Women should raise legs one at a time.

Concentrated Sit-Ups (T)

- Lie on your back with knees bent, feet flat on the floor. Place your hands on your temples and raise your head and shoulders off the floor.
- From this position raise your head and shoulders higher and hold for a count of 2.
- Return to the starting position and repeat. The head and shoulders should not touch the floor during this exercise. Keep your lower back on the floor throughout.

Advanced Dorsals (G)

This is a useful exercise for increasing flexibility and strengthening the lower back.
- Lie face down on the floor in the 'prime' position with arms outstretched in front, palms facing inwards.
- Raise your arms, upper body, legs and thighs off the floor.
- Return to the starting position and repeat. Keep the hips on the floor throughout.

Alternate Split Jumps (L)

- Stand erect with feet together.
- Jump on the spot, then jump again, landing with legs apart, the right leg forwards and the left leg backwards.

- Jump, landing with feet together.
- Jump the legs apart again, reversing the position of the legs.

- Repeat the alternate split jumps bringing alternate legs forwards. Make sure the trailing knee does not touch the floor and the leading knee does not go over the ankle.

ADDITIONAL EXERCISES

Bum Jumps (L)

You will need to use a sturdy chair or bench for this exercise. Choose the height according to your ability.

- Sit facing the back of the chair with your legs wide apart, hands holding on to the top of the chair.
- Still holding on to the chair, jump up on to the seat. Jump down again, bending your knees and then lowering your bottom on to the seat of the chair.
- Repeat.

Ski Jumps (L)

For this exercise use a bench, broom handle or pole balanced between two chairs. Start off with a low height and adjust the height according to your ability.

- Stand sideways on to the pole, feet together, knees slightly bent.
- Jump sideways over the pole, moving your feet slightly apart as you jump. Always remember to bend the knees on landing.
- Stand erect again, before jumping sideways over the pole to return to the other side.
- Repeat.
- To make the exercise easier at first, you can do a 'double bounce' between sides. The fitter you are, the less you will need to pause between jumps.

Calf Raises (L)

This exercise puts the calf muscles through their full range of movement.

● Stand facing and holding on to the back of a chair with your heels on the floor and your toes raised on a plank of wood no more than 2 inches thick. This helps to stretch the calf muscles more.

● Rise on to the balls of your feet and then lower your heels back to the floor.

● Repeat.

ADDITIONAL EXERCISES

Side Leg Raises (L)

- Stand facing the back of a chair and rest your fingers lightly on top of it.
- Raise your right leg directly out to the side. Keep your supporting leg straight, but do not lock the knee, and keep your hips level. Hold the raised position for a count of 2. Then lower the leg, returning it to the starting position, and repeat.
- Turn around and repeat with the other leg. Do an equal number of repetitions with each leg.

Backward Leg Raises (L)

- Start in the same position as the Side Leg Raise.
- Raise your right leg to the back. Again, try to keep your hips level. Hold the raised position for a count of 2. Then lower the leg, returning it to the starting position, and repeat.
- Repeat with the other leg.

ADDITIONAL EXERCISES

Forward Leg Raises

- Stand sideways on to the chair and hold it lightly with your left hand. Bend the supporting leg and raise the right leg out in front, keeping your hips level. Hold the raised position for a count of 2. Then lower the leg, returning it to the starting position, and repeat.
- Turn around and repeat with the other leg.

Hamstring Curls (L)

- Stand erect with feet together and face the back of a chair. Rest your fingertips lightly on top.
- Keeping your knees together, raise the lower part of your right leg to the back at an angle of 90 degrees. Hold the raised position for a count of 2. Then lower the leg, returning it to the starting position, and repeat.
- Repeat with the other leg.

Quadriceps Raises (L)

- Sit on a chair with your back straight, knees bent, feet flat on the floor.
- Keeping your knees together, raise the right leg straight out in front with your foot flexed. Hold the raised position for a count of 2. Then lower the leg, returning it to the starting position, and repeat.
- Repeat with the other leg.

Alternatives to Daily Routine

To work out exact equivalents for different exercise taken and sports played makes converting Chaos Theory into a simple equation look easy. You cannot say playing squash for 45 minutes equals a 5 mile run without taking into account the skill of both players. So what follows is only an approximate guide. Basically if you play a sport hard and fast, so that you get your heart rate up, the blood flowing and the sweat dripping, it is doing you good.

For some people a change is as good as a rest and certainly for me variation in my exercise diet is vital to keeping up my enthusiasm. Most of the exercises in the Royal Marines Total Fitness Programme are inherently solitary in their execution and unlike a batch of recruits, you will be doing it either alone or with one mate. Chances are that you have been getting rather anti-social! Most sports involve a strong social element, so a quick visit to the local squash or aerobics club might do you more than just heart racing good.

The following is only a rough guide:

R = Run
Y = Yomp
C = Circuit
B = Cycle
S = Swim

Badminton – played for at least 45 minutes with people of equal or better standard. (R, B)

Squash – played for at least 45 minutes with people of equal or better standard. (R, B)

Tennis – 60–90 minutes of singles, 2 hours doubles. (R, B)

Volleyball – hard game. (R, B)

Soccer – indoor 5-a-side. (R, B)

Rugby – sevens – there is a lot of hanging around in the full game. (R, B)

Hockey – full game played at pace or 7-a-side. (R, B)

Basketball – game or 30 minutes fast one on one. (R, B)

Golf – provided you play 18 holes, carry the bag yourself and walk fast between strokes! (Y)

Rowing – either on river or on machine. (C, Y)

Cricket – while professional cricketers are very fit, for the amateurs it sadly does very little except it can relax the brain while also requiring immense concentration.

Water polo – a hard brutal game even when played for fun. (S, C)

Aerobics/Step aerobics – 45 minute work out. (R, C, B) For step aerobics, make sure you have a good instructor to avoid Achilles tendon and knee injuries.

Skiing – full day. (R, Y)

Weight training – By all means pop down to the gym after you have reached Level 3, but weight training is highly specialized so always get the instructor to show you around all the different machines and, if you are concentrating on free weights, using the right technique. For the Royal Marines Total Fitness Programme the object is not to look like Arnold Schwarzenegger (among the Corps there is debate that despite – or perhaps because of – his physique and familiarity with high-tech killing machines he might not be able to pass the Commando Tests). The aim is to build strength not bulk, so keep the weights light and concentrate on endurance. Do lots of repetitions (12–20) of a smaller weight, then take a breather and do it again. While adopting a Whole Body Approach you should concentrate more on the legs and on those parts of the body you feel are weakest when you are carrying a pack. (Y)

Dancing – don't laugh. Professional dancers constantly prove to have more all round fitness than many athletes. Dance training takes care of stretching, mobility and gives a full body workout. A natural sense of rhythm helps. (All)

Horse riding – A good hour's gallop, taking in a few jumps will work out both legs and upper body. (C)

Wind surfing – a rough sea and a high wind will work out both legs and can put heavy strain on upper body. However you have to learn first. (C, Y)

Clay pigeon shooting – see cricket.

Bungee jumping – it does get the heart pounding – but so fast you go anaerobic.

Synchronized swimming – it may look silly but it is very hard work. It is also extremely difficult for men, as their fat content means they tend to sink. (S)

Whatever competitive sport you are playing, try to do it with people technically a bit better than you, especially in ball games. Your superior fitness will close that gap very quickly. This means your opponent will have to try harder to win. He or she will enjoy it more and you will get better, so everyone goes home happy.

Treating Minor Injuries

The *Rice* Cure for Minor Muscular Injuries

RICE is the most underrated way of treating minor injuries to yourself. It stands for:

Rest – rest injured limb, or whole body if advised, until the treatment is complete.

Ice – apply an ice pack to the injured area for 10 minutes every hour possible for 48 hours. This reduces bleeding from torn blood vessels.

Compression – bandage the injury firmly (but not so tightly as to reduce blood flow) in order to contain the swelling. Use anti-inflammatory drugs from the chemist after consulting your doctor.

Elevation – elevate injured limb. This allows blood to flow towards the heart. This reduces the pressure of fluid on the injured area.

If the injury persists see a doctor.

When you start training again, do so at a lower level. With aerobic training, research shows that you can take no exercise for three weeks and lose a minimal amount of fitness, after that it increases dramatically. If the injury threatens to be long term, wherever possible exercise the other parts of the body – keeping fit should speed your recovery time. But don't be a fool and try too hard too soon; further aggravating an injury could mean months not weeks out of action.